Reflections:
Images and Memories

2017 Pamlico Writers' Group
Anthology

Published by: Pamlico Writers' Group

For information, please contact:

Pamlico Writer's Group
150 West Main Street
Washington, NC 27889

Email: pamlicowritersgroup@gmail.com

ISBN-10: 978-1979093156

ISBN-13: 1979093156

Printed in the United States of America

Pamlico Writers' Group Anthologies

Showboat (2000)

Showboat II (2002)

A Carolina Christmas (2016)

Reflections (2017)

Foreword

By Elaine Lettick
Poet Laureate Chairperson

When poet Jerry Cuthrell founded the Pamlico Writers' Group in 1973, it consisted of a small group of writers determined to establish an organization to encourage and nurture writers to achieve their dreams. Mr. Cuthrell would be proud that the group now boasts eighty-one members from all over Eastern North Carolina. Some have written and published books of their own; others have been inspired to resurrect works long forgotten. Many have come and gone, but the *Pamlico Writers' Group* stands as a beacon of hope to future writers and their dreams. It continues in its commitment to provide writers with tools and resources through its semi-monthly critique groups, monthly writing competitions, annual conferences, and varied workshops. Additionally, to honor the memory of its founder, the group recently launched a search for the first-ever *Heart of the Pamlico Poet Laureate* to represent all of Eastern North Carolina.

This year's anthology, *Reflections: Images and Memories*, is a collection of exemplary writing by our members and future members. The prose and poetry in this volume represent a collage of work by published authors and emerging writers. Pamlico Writers' Group is particularly honored to include prose and poetry from high school students—young emerging writers to whom we entrust our future.

Each writer whose work is included in the anthology has expertly crafted a piece around his or her own interpretation of this year's theme—*Reflections: Images and Memories*. The collection is the culmination of hard work and truly affirms the group's commitment to its mission. With this anthology, The Pamlico Writers' Group is proud to deliver its finest product to date.

Our Reflections

By Sherri Hollister
Chair, Pamlico Writer's Group

Through reflections, like the face of the moon's silver glow on the Pamlico or the sunlight's dappled drops of golden light, we along the river's edge can view the passing of time in the ebb and flow of the tides. Our native history lives on in our farmers, loggers, watermen, and hunters. Though times have changed all around us, many things here in rural North Carolina have stayed the same. Like our tar-heeled ancestors, we often dig in and remain—even when change might be easier, even preferable.

When I first started with the Pamlico Writers' Group over fifteen years ago, I was unsure of my craft, believing it only to be a hobby. On and off again, I returned to the group over the years, gleaning information and struggling to write amid the chaos of a busy household. As my children grew and left home, I devoted more and more time to the dream of writing professionally. A few years ago, I came out to friends and family, announcing "I am a writer!"

Once the gauntlet has been laid down, it is challenging to then produce a work worthy of publishing. I have been on the cusp many times, struggling to have my work recognized. With the birth of the Pamlico Writers' Group 2016 Anthology, *A Carolina Christmas*, my dream of being published finally came true.

The effort to produce a book worthy of being published takes time and effort, and dedicated people. This year's anthology, *Reflections*, was a labor of love. Louis Edwards, Pamlico Writers' Group assistant chairperson, designed the cover. The theme was chosen by a committee vote with the hopes that the stories and poems would be varied and reflective of each author's individual interpretation of the idea.

The Pamlico Writers' Group has evolved from friends getting together to discuss their writing, to a serious group of talented writers sharing information, sharing their work, and assisting each other in becoming the best writers they can be.

When Doris Schneider first brought the idea of the Pamlico Writers' Conference to Jim Keen, the chairperson of the Pamlico

Writers' Group, they could not have conceived of the changes the conference would have on the group. With each conference, we challenge ourselves to greater diversity and expansion. We have hosted some of the greatest writers and poets in North Carolina as keynote speakers and presenters: Jill McCorkle, Sharyn McCrumb, Zelda Lockhart and Shelby Stephenson, just to name a few. We have met writers, agents, and publishers who have led workshops and spoken at luncheons. We have had award-winning presenters who have given blurbs for our anthologies, acted as judges, and served as mentors to our group. As the conference grew and morphed to become respected statewide, our group has become the place to be in Eastern North Carolina if you are a serious writer.

Some upcoming highlights:

February 3rd, 2018 the Pamlico Writers' Group will announce their first Heart of the Pamlico Poet Laureate at the Turnage Theater with live performances by the top five finalists.

March 23rd, 2018 will launch our Sixth Annual Pamlico Writers' Conference with keynote speaker Shelby Stephenson, North Carolina Poet Laureate.

March 24th, 2018 our Sixth Annual Pamlico Writers' Conference, "Shape Shifting Your Writing: Transforming Your Writing for Other Successful Markets."

For more information on the Pamlico Writers' Group, our Conference, or to become a member go to our:

Website: www.pamlicowritersgroup.org

Facebook: https://www.facebook.com/pamlicowritersgroup/

Twitter: https://twitter.com/pamlicowritersc?lang=en

Table of Contents

Acknowledgements

This anthology has been a group effort. One person says I have an idea and another says let's do this, and another adds their part until we have a finished product. Those people are Jim Keen, Doris Schneider, Sherri Hollister, Louis Edwards, and Jeanne Julian. Without you guys, this would still just be an idea.

Edited by Jeanne Julian and Doris Schneider
Cover design by Louis Edwards
Formatted by James Keen

2017 Reflections Competition

This is the new annual juried writing contest, featuring adult and student authors, with the specific purpose of publishing winning entries in our annual anthology. The competition is a replacement for the annual Writers Competition held annually since 2013.

First, Second, and Honorable Mention Prizes were awarded in the Adult competition while a student Poetry and Prose prizes were awarded.

Author Biography

Diane de Echeandia

Diane de Echeandia is a native North Carolinian, born in Wilmington, North Carolina. She writes poetry, short stories, and creative non-fiction. Diane has won awards in competitions sponsored by Christopher Newport University, the North Carolina Writers' Workshop in Asheville, NC, and the Pamlico Writers' Conference. Her poetry has appeared in SUNY Delhi's publication, *Agate*; *Art Inspires Poetry: An Anthology of Ekphrastic Poetry* 2015, 2016; *A Carolina Christmas Anthology,* 2016; *Skinny Poetry,* 8/16; and online magazines *Eskimopi,* and *Bindweed,* February 2017. Diane has enjoyed teaching ESL to college students and refugees. She lives in New Bern, NC.

Reflections Competition
Fiction First Place

Revelation from Climbing Tai Shan

By Diane de Echeandia

"I went looking for adventure and romance, and so I found them...
but I found also something I had never expected. I found a new self."
--Somerset Maughan

"Nobody said it was going to be easy," Fernando reminded me, as my calf muscles burned. This was not the winding, rugged mountain path I had expected. We had to make our way up 7,000 ancient stone steps, carved out 3,000 years ago during the reign of Emperor Shih-Huang, who is known for having begun construction of the Great Wall.

"I can't believe I'm doing this," I moaned, pausing to survey the steps ascending ahead.

The steps were not smooth and were of unequal heights, so I had to adjust constantly. The entire ascent amounted to more than six miles (or about 10,000 meters) to the top. Mount Tai Shan, the most sacred of China's five holy mountains, is associated with the rising sun. According to Taoist beliefs, the rising sun signifies birth and renewal. As the hours wore on, and weariness set in, it was hard to think about birth and renewal, although I could have used a good dose of both.

It was around 8:00 pm and the four of us (three students at Tianjin University and I, a visiting teacher there) had been climbing since dusk. I tried to remember whose idea this trip was, and why I had agreed to go. What was I thinking? To walk up stone steps through half the night, starting at dusk, just to see the sunrise from the summit of Tai Shan was a monumental task—the most strenuous activity I had ever done. Tai Shan means "Tranquil Mountain," but tranquil didn't come close to describing how I felt.

"This was your idea, wasn't it, Fernando?"

"You got that right. Are we having fun yet?"

"Hardly." I took a swig from my water bottle. I had learned that Fernando was the ultimate tourist who took advantage of every opportunity to see China's historic sights. He told me he had recently convinced some of his classmates to tour the home-place of Confucius and had also led excursions to Beijing to see Tiananmen Square and the Forbidden City.

* * * * *

It was spring, 1997. I had decided that a semester teaching English in China would provide me with a useful foreign teaching experience that I could add to my résumé. Well, that's not the whole truth. The *real* reason for this trip was that my two-year relationship with Kyle had abruptly stalled, and I desperately needed a change of scene. I wanted to get away as far as possible from everything that reminded me of him. I had believed he was the love of my life, and we had discussed marriage. I was shocked and devastated by his sudden declaration on our way home after dinner. He had looked at me sadly, and out of nowhere said, "I think we need to spend some time apart."

"What? Where is this coming from?" I asked. "What's going on? Have you met someone else?"

"No. There's no one else. I just need some space," he stammered without looking at me directly.

"Space? Space for what?"

"To think. I can't explain it now. I'm not sure I'm ready to get married again. I'm sorry. I'll call you."

My attempts to get him to discuss his reasons failed, as did my suggestion that we didn't have to get married anytime soon. Kyle had never been able to express his feelings very well, but his vague responses before he drove away that night was unsatisfying and left me feeling baffled, angry, and hurt.

After he had walked me to the door and left, I entered my house feeling like I had just been sucker-punched. I remembered a friend who came home from work to find that her live-in boyfriend and all his furniture and personal things were gone. He had left her a goodbye note taped to the refrigerator door! I could take some comfort—I guess—that at least Kyle had told me face-to-face. Not that I found it any less painful. I was emotionally wounded. I longed for answers. Why didn't I see this coming?

Now what? A week passed, and then two, and Kyle didn't call. The one good thing about his abrupt departure was that there were only two weeks left in the semester at the college where I had been teaching for several years. I stumbled through, giving exams and calculating grades. I felt out of focus and moved as if in slow motion. Christmas break was looming, and then spring semester. I had to do something to pull myself together before my sadness developed into a full-blown clinical depression.

During the semester break, while browsing an educational website, I saw an ad for a teacher of English as a Foreign Language for the spring semester in China at Tianjin University, ninety miles south of Beijing. This could be just what I needed—a chance to get away, do some traveling, and gain foreign teaching experience. I made a hasty decision and responded to the ad. I soon received a reply and an official invitation to join the faculty of Tianjin University as a visiting teacher from the U.S. I requested a leave of absence from the English Department and started packing. I had been scheduled to teach only two classes, and there were a number of adjunct teachers who were available to fill in for me. My hope was that the teaching experience in China would provide me with a much-needed distraction which would diffuse my anger and sadness and give me a clearer perspective. I knew this was avoidance, and wouldn't resolve anything between Kyle and me. Nevertheless, I felt compelled to go. Without telling Kyle my plans—assuming he didn't care anyway—I left for China.

* * * * *

There we were, on the mountain—a typical international group: Fernando, from New York City via Argentina; Pham, from Vietnam; Lilly, from China; and me, Ann, from Virginia. I had learned about this trip to Tai Shan from Lilly. I didn't know Pham at all, but I had seen Fernando around the campus. I'd spoken to him several times as he was one of a handful of Americans studying at the university. Unable to convince any of my colleagues to join us, I decided to go with the students. I felt I was capable of keeping up with the group, despite being forty-something. I was physically fit and had always enjoyed hiking.

"Pham, what's the hurry?" I yelled. "Slow down!" I was beginning to think I wasn't so fit after all.

"Yeah, we've got all night!" Fernando shouted, out of breath. Our pleas were ignored as Pham seemed hell-bent on racing to the top.

Pham, a slightly built, fidgety fellow, and Lilly, his new girlfriend of a few weeks, were at least 50 yards ahead of Fernando and me. Lilly, our Chinese spokesperson, was essential since most Chinese people spoke no English. Usually, only urban shopkeepers, hotel or restaurant staff, and university students could speak English. The other three of us didn't speak much Chinese beyond shopping vocabulary. Lilly, quiet by nature, took very seriously her self-appointed job of being our guide on this journey. She was a large-boned girl, a few inches taller than Pham, and a competent leader. Pham, on the other hand, acted as if he had done this trip before, always walking way ahead of us, as if he knew exactly where he was going. I wondered if he thought he could impress Lilly by acting as if he had the situation under control, knowing full well he was totally dependent on her, just as Fernando and I were.

Fernando, the big guy, was the formidable group member. He rarely smiled, and had a gruff demeanor, but was surprisingly good-natured and likable. He had grown up in Argentina but had survived years of living in the Bronx. His outfit of choice was an oversized faded tee shirt with the sleeves cut out, baggy sweat pants, and high-top sneakers. With his shaved head and intense glare, he could have been mistaken for a skinhead. I was impressed that he had come to Tianjin University to study Chinese, and I was beginning to appreciate his quest for adventure and discovery.

Only a few hours ago—though it now seemed like days—in Tianjin, we had boarded the train for the journey to Tai An, the small town at the foot of the mountain. We had arrived at the train station in Tianjin early and bought our tickets. Like Americans do, we lined up between the metal bars beside the track hoping to be the first to board and get good seats. We felt lucky until all of a sudden, Fernando yelled "Holy shit!" Loud voices followed as hoards of people converged on the scene. Some were carrying huge cloth-covered bundles; there were mothers with babies, old people, and factory workers returning home for the weekend—all pushing and shoving each other, and us.

"Watch out!" Lilly cautioned. "Stay together." Masses of people jumped over the guard rails and each other, pushing forward. By the time the train arrived and screeched to a stop, we had been trod over and pushed to the back of the mob. We were last to board the train! So much for queuing up. I was aware that people did not line up as we do in the States, but this crush was shocking and scary.

Obviously, these people knew something we didn't. When we finally boarded the train, there were no seats left.

"Oh no. What are we going to do now?" I asked, looking to Lilly for an answer. I couldn't envision standing for hours while the train lumbered along through the countryside. People sat on the floor in the cramped spaces between cars, or sat cross-legged in the aisles, resting on their bundles, smoking. Toddlers routinely squatted on the floor to relieve themselves.

The passengers stared at our little group. We were used to being stared at because we looked different from the Chinese with our light hair color and round eyes. They rarely saw foreigners in the countryside—let alone on this train. Foreigners were found mostly in Beijing, Xian, Shanghai, or other large cities popular with tourists.

Lilly spoke to a porter, who miraculously found us a table for four in the dining car, where we stayed for the duration of the trip.

"Thank goodness we can sit down. Thank goodness for Lilly!" I exclaimed as we flung our backpacks to the floor. Pham and Fernando nodded in agreement. During the ride, Fernando paid rapt attention to Chairman Mao's *Little Red Book*, which he was reading. I concentrated on the dining car bill-of-fare. The menu consisted of Ramen noodles and tea, served by a woman who walked around the dining car and poured boiling water from a heavy metal tea kettle on request. Pham and Lilly spent their time trying to form intelligible sentences in English in order to communicate with each other, while I put my head down on my folded arms and napped.

* * * * *

As we continued our walk up the mountain, it was getting darker and colder, and we were weary. Even with his strapping physique, Fernando had to take frequent rest breaks, and I happily joined him.

"Look at their shoes," Fernando said. We sat on the sloping stone wall that ran beside the steps and observed people making their way to the top. They were wearing a variety of shoe styles, totally unsuitable for hiking or any type of athletic activity. Most of the women were wearing leather sandals with two-inch stacked heels. The men wore leather lace-up shoes.

"I know. Maybe China exports everything it makes, or maybe the people have no taste for athletic shoes." I wondered aloud.

"Maybe they can't afford them."

Most of the younger men were wearing the ubiquitous flimsy, gray or brown polyester suit jacket, and the elderly men were clothed in the traditional Mao jacket. Many women wore pant suits that were fashionable in the U.S. decades ago, or they wore long cotton or silk skirts. No one was wearing khakis or any type of suitable hiking gear. We were the only people wearing shorts and carrying backpacks loaded with snacks, bottled water, and flashlights.

"Even though we're the only foreigners in sight on the mountain, no one is staring at us," I whispered. "That feels good for a change!"

"Uh huh, it does," Fernando responded. He paused to catch his breath. "These people are focused. Notice they aren't talking? They couldn't care less about us."

Other climbers were clearly on a spiritual mission. Many people stopped to pray at the small shrines strategically placed along the path. Our motives for being here were obviously different from the motives of these earnest people, who may have waited a lifetime to make this sacred pilgrimage. The seriousness of their journey made our reason for climbing the mountain seem shallow.

"Look at all the elderly people out here," Fernando observed. "I can't imagine my grandparents doing this."

"Me neither." We were both impressed with the number of pilgrims spanning several generations, walking all night to pay respect to the holy mountain.

I was beginning to feel self-conscious. This trip had begun for me as an excuse to keep my mind off Kyle. It started out as anything but a spiritual journey, but now I wondered. The higher we climbed, the more I pondered the significance of the journey for myself. With each difficult step up the mountain, I began to evaluate my relationship with Kyle and question my actions with him. I hadn't accepted the possibility that he wasn't ready for a long-term commitment. Why hadn't I seen that our needs were out of sync?

Instead of drawing him nearer, I had pushed him away. Harboring these thoughts, I tried to focus on the climb and our surroundings.

"I would like to know what this writing is about," I remarked, as we passed huge stone tablets with Chinese writings on them. As we continued walking, I noted that the walls lining the path were covered with flowing lines of artfully hand-carved Chinese words. "It's frustrating not to be able to read anything. Where is Lilly?" I grumbled. "How did she and Pham get so far ahead of us?"

When we had begun our climb at the foot of the mountain, our clothes were damp with sweat. But the air got cooler at the higher elevations, which we hadn't prepared for. We were beginning to feel the crisp, chilly air. Around the fourth hour of climbing, we saw lights and heard loud, excited voices above us.

"I wonder what's going on?" Fernando panted as he quickened his pace.

"I don't know. It sounds like a TV."

We climbed a few more steps and came upon a flat area with a small stone house in the center. Three young Chinese men were sitting outside on white plastic chairs smoking cigarettes and watching a basketball game on a small black-and-white TV. They were cheering and having a sporting good time.

"Do they actually live here? How in the heck did they get TV reception up here?" I wondered aloud.

"Ann, look! It's the NBA! They're watching a game between the Lakers and the Celtics!" Fernando exclaimed, moving closer to the group.

Taking advantage of this as an opportunity to rest, we hung out for a few minutes with the three basketball fans. The guys did not appear surprised at our sudden appearance, and after exchanging friendly "Ni haos" (hellos), we temporarily became part of their group. We joined them in cheering for the teams, but were awed by watching American television on Tai Shan! When we began shivering in the cold mountain air, we thanked them and moved on with the Celtics two points ahead.

"How much farther do you think it is?" I asked, knowing full well Fernando didn't have a clue how far it was to our destination: the summit and a cozy inn.

"It can't be too much farther. We've been walking since 6:30, and we're supposed to be there around midnight. It's now 10:30."

"I don't know about you, but I'm about ready to drop, and I'm freezing. All I want to do is sit down."

"Come on, Ann. You can do this. We've come this far. We've got to keep going."

The thoughts of shelter and a warm bed beckoned to me, so I shut up and trudged along behind Fernando. The wind had picked up, and our thin jackets provided little protection. Finally, after two more hours of walking, we saw a crudely-built two-story stone structure on the horizon with lots of Chinese people milling around outside. We had reached the top of the mountain.

"Yay, we can get a room and sleep!" I yelled.

A moment later, we caught up with Pham and Lilly, who didn't look as happy as we felt.

"Did we get a room?" I asked, pulling my polyester jacket tighter while dancing around to keep warm.

"How much does it cost?" Fernando inquired, unzipping his backpack to search for money.

"No rooms." Pham stated. Both he and Lilly were looking grim.

"What do you mean?" We both shouted in disbelief.

"All full. We can sleep outside," Lilly responded, as though this were the expected and normal thing to do.

"What? Sleep outside? Where?" We glared at our companions, and then at the hard stone ground surrounding the "hotel," while the frigid wind stung our faces and whipped our bare legs.

Just then, out of nowhere, as if he had overheard and understood our conversation, a man showed up pulling a wagon-load of Chinese army coats for rent. Eyeing our plight and desperation, and being a clever entrepreneur, he spoke words we clearly understood, "Wu" (five yuan, which was less than a dollar). After paying him, he doled out the heavy army-green full-length military coats.

We hastily put the coats on, and looking around, realized we were now dressed like everyone else who was stranded on the mountaintop unable to get a room in the inn. The coats were incredibly warm, with a brown fleece collar, thick lining and buttons up the front. The right sleeve displayed a prominent red star. At that point, who cared if the coats were leftovers from the Chinese Communist army? All around us, people wearing identical coats were beginning to bed down on the hard rocky surface, as if this were something they did every night. Since we had no choice, our little band joined the crowd, each of us searching out a suitable rock that would offer some shelter from the harsh wind.

"What happens in the morning?" I yelled over to Fernando, who was looking uncomfortable a few rocks away.

"Lilly said someone will wake everybody up just before the sun rises," he hollered back from his hot-dog-bun-shaped rock.

"Great," I answered sarcastically. The mere thought of being awakened at dawn made me angry. By this time Pham and Lilly had cozied up nearby, huddled together.

My mind drifted to Kyle and our last time together. I had hoped for a pleasant evening with him after dinner in front of the fireplace. Instead, out of nowhere, he announced he needed some space! Well this is some space, all right! With these depressing thoughts, I wrapped my military regulation-issue coat around my body and, with my backpack for a pillow, closed my eyes and fell asleep.

At dawn, I was awakened by loud and not-so-friendly male voices shouting something unintelligible in Chinese which must have meant "Get up" because that's what everyone was doing. I saw several men scurrying around nudging people awake and pointing with excitement at the sky. Everywhere people were emerging from their cocoons like large, green caterpillars. My bones ached from the hard stony surface, and I wasn't ready to leave the warmth of my rented coat, wet with dew, to return it in the chilly, damp morning air.

"Hurry up," Fernando called to me. He, Lilly, and Pham started following a line of people moving single-file up a small rocky knoll. At that moment, I didn't care about seeing the sun rise over Mt. Tai Shan. I just wanted to stay put and keep warm. But as the crowd began moving with more energy, I was motivated by a fear of getting separated from my group. I scrambled on leaden legs up the hill to join them.

"Over here, Miss Ann," Lilly called, motioning furiously when I reached the summit. People were everywhere, sitting on top of rocks, hills, and dirt piles with their cameras in hand, poised for the big moment. The foggy air started to clear, and the sky began to brighten, as the tip of reddish-orange sun crept above the horizon. When the sun fully exposed itself, the energy of the crowd was palpable as we heard murmurs of excitement and clicks of camera shutters. People all around were requesting snapshots of themselves seeming to hold the sun in the palm of their hands. Caught up in the moment, we did likewise and clicked away, shooting pictures of the sun and each other.

"This is the most amazing sunrise I've ever seen," Fernando said quietly.

"I agree. It's lovely. I'm so glad we did this." I looked over at Lilly and Pham, who were holding hands, which made me lonely for Kyle. It was inspiring to see so many awestruck people sharing a common experience together. Differences in language, religion, and culture didn't matter at that moment. We were united in our appreciation of this natural event and the harmony it created on this day, in this place.

As we began our descent, I thought of Kyle. Sadness overwhelmed me. He should be here to share this with me. I missed him and felt an urgent need to speak to him. I realized I couldn't continue to avoid confronting the reasons for our breakup. I made a decision to call him as soon as we got back to campus. I heard Fernando yell, "What's your hurry, Ann?"

"I've got to get back. I've got something important to do."

"Miss Ann," Lilly called. "Did you like the sunrise?"

"Yes, it was wonderful. I'm so happy you told me about this trip."

"Me too." Lilly smiled and turned to catch up with Pham, who was heading down the steps.

It was a perfect day, with the sun shining in a cloudless blue sky. We were surrounded by distant mountain ranges that reminded me of the mountains seen in Chinese silk paintings. The mountains were slender and green with jagged profiles that looked nothing like mountains in the U.S. We could see homes with ornate architecture and bright colors, perched here and there on the mountainsides.

"This scenery is magnificent," I marveled, stopping to take pictures. "We couldn't see any of this last night."

Fernando agreed. "I'm so glad we can see this in the daytime. Look at what we missed!"

We later learned that the stone tablets along the path contained poems from the third millennium praising the beauty of the surroundings which we couldn't fully see when we were climbing at night. Our only sources of light had been our flashlights and the moonlight.

"The atmosphere going down the mountain is so different from last night. Notice how people are smiling and talking to each other now?"

"Yeah, I guess they're happy they made it to the top, and are now on their way back down—mission accomplished."

The hike down took about half the time it took to climb up but still had its challenges.

"Do your knees hurt?" Fernando asked, rubbing his left knee.

"Yes, both knees do. I think walking *down* steps is harder on the knees than walking up."

As the temperature rose, we started shedding outer layers of clothing. When we got to the foot of the mountain, mid-afternoon, we were hot, tired and grateful to be at the bottom.

We headed to the train station for the trip home, where we bought food and drinks and looked for empty benches. Exhausted, we each staked out a place to rest in the crowded station. The train was scheduled to arrive in two hours. I noticed this time people *were* staring at us, but I was so tired, I couldn't have cared less. Since I had a whole wooden bench to myself, I put my feet up, stretched out, and slept.

* * * * *

The train ride back to Tianjin was uneventful and much less crowded than before. While Lily and Pham chatted nearby, and Fernando dozed, I rehearsed the phone conversation I planned to have with Kyle.

When we arrived back on campus, I said goodbye to my hiking partners and headed for the nearest pay phone. Kyle and I hadn't communicated since before I left. But now I had to take action, even if I had to face the possibility of another rejection. I would be returning home soon and dreaded resuming my life as I had left it. I dialed his number and waited. The phone rang several times, and just as I was about to hang up, he answered.

"Hello. Kyle here."

"Hello, Kyle. This is Ann. How are you?"

"Ann, it's good to hear your voice. I'm fine...except for missing you."

Unable to sound nonchalant, I blurted out, "I miss you, too. We need to talk."

"When are you coming home? Your friends told me you went to China, but I didn't know how to get in touch with you. I figured you didn't want to talk to me anyway." He sounded sincere.

"I'll be leaving here in three weeks. My flight from Beijing lands at JFK. I have a connecting flight to Norfolk."

"Give me your flight information, and I'll be there to pick you up. We've got a lot to talk about," he said.

"Okay, I'll send you my flight schedule. Can't wait to see you. My phone card is about to run out, so I've got to hang up now." After hurried goodbyes, I put the receiver on the hook and sat down, feeling tension leave my body. Excited and hopeful, I took a long walk in the park on campus and relived our phone conversation word for word.

* * * * *

During the flight home, as I reflected on my time in China, I felt certain that I had done the right thing. I had given Kyle several months without me, and time for myself to reevaluate our relationship. In retrospect, I probably was expecting too much from Kyle, too soon. He clearly had a fear of commitment since his divorce. I would back off and accept it.

And maybe I had taken away something from Mt. Tai Shan. Whether it was the sight of the sunrise, the earnestness of the Chinese climbers, or making it to the top of the sacred mountain, it didn't really matter. Possibly it had something to do with the sun's effect on birth and renewal. Perhaps it was all of the above. As I reclined my seat and settled back for the long flight, I closed my eyes and imagined returning to China one day. And the next time, maybe I would bring Kyle.

Author Biography

Dennis Listermann-Vierling

I am a former social studies teacher and retired Greek Orthodox priest. My wife and I moved from California to Washington, North Carolina, in June of 2017. My hobbies include puppetry, gardening, and writing. My only published writings have been limited to parish histories and family genealogy books. However, I have written a number of fiction stories in my spare time. Now that I am semiretired, I hope to devote more time to writing.

Reflections Competition
Fiction Second Place

Never Fear the Dead

By Dennis Listermann-Vierling

Autumn winds of late October aimlessly blew a swirl of fading reddish leaves around a row of twisted crape myrtles. The tree-lined East 2nd Street featured a row of quaint Victorian homes in the sleepy southern town of Washington, North Carolina. However, the nearby business district, like the spread of kudzu, had been slowly creeping into this historic neighborhood and some of these grand homes had been converted into offices. Such was the case for one elegant old structure which glimmered in the late afternoon sunlight. It was a stately, gleaming white mansion with four immense ionic columns surrounded by a low columned wall.

"Gee, this place gives me the creeps. Didn't some stiff once hang himself from the chandelier?" a voice whispered as he glanced up at the dangling crystal light fixture.

"Don't be a baby," his companion chuckled as he closed the creaky front door. "From what the guide said on the Ghost Tour, that was decades ago. Besides, you should never fear the dead."

Doug Pickett frowned, unconvinced. Turning around, he stepped back with a startle as he stared up at the menacing statue of a man with the head of a dog with sharp pointed ears.

His companion laughed. "Don't be stupid—this place is cool. That's a statue of Anubis, the Guardian of the Dead.'

Clay Cutler, ever since he was a kid growing up, had an abiding love for Ancient Egypt. His clear blue eyes sparkled as the Washington High School junior looked around the dimly lit foyer. The whole museum, a recently converted mansion built in the Victorian Age, was filled with brightly painted reliefs of the long-dead kings, stone images of the animal gods and even the furniture that the ancient peoples used in their daily lives over 2,000 years ago. The experience this afternoon caused him to feel as if he were a time traveler transported back to the wondrous age of the pharaohs.

Doug, a lanky fellow classmate, tugged nervously at his sleeve, "Let's get out of here. We have a ton of homework and should head home."

Clay shook his head. "You go—I want to stay a little longer."

His friend shrugged. "Okay, man—suit yourself. I'll see you at school tomorrow."

Doug turned and left. Clay proceeded through a portal constructed like a temple pylon. The red-headed teenager found himself in an adjoining chamber built to resemble a temple of some sort. It was very dark. The ceiling to floor windows had been papered over. The only light came from a bronze brazier with a tiny flame burning in front of a wall with a series of engravings which stretched from the floor to the ceiling. From what he could tell, there appeared to be two rows of stone pillars topped with capitals resembling lotus flowers. He moved past the columns toward the etching but could not find a brief explanation of what he was looking at.

"Good afternoon, young man," a voice quietly murmured in a slightly foreign-accented English.

Clay, with a start, swung around. He found himself before a thin, pale old gentleman quietly standing with his hands lightly clasped. The stranger had an exotic air about him. A tasseled red fez sat on his grey head while he wore a crisp white suite with an old-fashioned gold pocket watch which could be seen hanging neatly from his vest. He smelled of incense yet seemed to the seventeen-year-old teenager to somehow belong to this place.

"Afternoon," Clay grunted with a belated smile. "The sign on the front gate said to come in and look around. I was just admiring this exhibit, but the light is bad."

The old gentleman smiled, revealing a row of worn yellow teeth. "Ah, I was in the back cataloging some newly acquired artifacts. It's a pleasure to welcome visitors and show off my collection of Egyptian antiquities. Let me move the brazier closer."

As the youth stepped aside, the elderly gentleman scooted the brazier closer to the wall. As he did so, the dim images on the wall came into clearer focus. "Do you know who this central relief is of?" the old man asked politely.

Clay nodded as he studied the wall carving. "Yes. It is of Osiris, the god of the dead. He was depicted with green skin because green is the color of living plants and is a sign of life. It was a reminder to the ancient Egyptians that Osiris, though killed by his brother Set, was brought to life again by his wife Isis."

The elderly gentleman, tapping his fingertips in approval, quietly bowed his head. "You are correct young man. Isis performed the sacred rituals and chanted the sacred spells over the body of Osiris which brought him back from the dead. I take it then that you are an enthusiast of Ancient Egypt?"

The red-headed teenager grinned sheepishly. "Yes, I guess so." Clay confessed, "I've been interested in history for years and my favorite subject is Ancient Egypt. Little Washington has never had much luck with museums of any type. Thus, I was thrilled when a buddy of mine from school happened to tell me that a private museum about Ancient Egypt had actually opened up here. I could hardly wait to come in and see this exhibit. I take it that you work here?"

The old man stepped closer and raised his arm and pointed around. "*Oui*," he replied softly in French before switching back to English, "I am Professor Louis Delacroix. I am both the curator and owner of this museum. I am pleased that you came here to see my modest collection. I have been to Egypt countless times and have accumulated some interesting treasures over the years. Would you be interested in seeing the sarcophagus of Lord Neskhons Nebit? It is the centerpiece of my exhibit."

Clay's eyes widened in excitement. "Sure, that would be great!"

The old man smiled indulgently and waved for the teenager to follow. Exiting the room, the pair proceeded down a carpeted corridor framed by a series of niches. Inside each hollowed-out space was a stone bust. While some of the figures were depicted wearing a Nemes headdress, some looked oddly different.

"What are these?" Clay asked, "Some of these statues look almost Grecian."

The elderly curator nodded and smiled. "My dear sir, you are quite perceptive for one so young. Yes, these are busts of some of the Ptolemaic rulers of Egypt. They were a Macedonian dynasty, the last of the great families to rule over the Two Lands. The Great Cleopatra was the last sovereign to wear the double-headed crown."

Clay paused to look at one of the busts. It was a woman with hair tightly pulled up. Her expression was serene yet proud. He stooped and read the sign, which said, "Unknown woman. Ptolemaic Period (305-30 BC)."

"Hum, perhaps this was the face of old Cleo herself," he mused quietly.

The curator, pulling out a series of skeleton keys from his breast pocket, stopped at a closed door and unlocked it. The door's metallic hinges creaked mightily as the door swung open. "Wait here a moment," the old man asked as he stepped inside, "while I get us some light."

As Clay waited patiently, he heard the sound of a match strike. Within a short time, there was a soft glow in the doorway.

"Come in" the elderly professor called out.

Moving inside, Clay saw Professor Louis Delacroix holding a lit oil lamp. The vessel was made of clay and appeared to be an ancient artifact itself. "Wouldn't it be easier to install electric lights?" the young man asked.

The old man waved his arm dismissively. "Ah, that would spoil the effect. The purpose of a museum is to help recreate an atmosphere of the past as it was."

It took Clay a few moments for his eyes to adjust to the darkness. A heavy gloom seemed to hang over the windowless room. Gradually the young man's eyes adjusted to the dimness, allowing the teenager to make out his surroundings. He found himself in a rather cramped chamber. The room's walls were plastered over and painted with scenes of men and women working in the fields, of children playing along a marshy shoreline, and of hunters with spears cornering a hippopotamus in the river. In the center of the room, under a high vaulted ceiling painted with stars, lay a large granite sarcophagus. Incised along the sides were rows of hieroglyphic inscriptions. There appeared to be no stone lid.

"You recreated an authentic Egyptian tomb!" he blurted out. "It's like being in the Valley of the Kings!"

Walking to the stone tomb, the curator beckoned to the youth to follow. "I'm glad you like it." The professor replied affably. "Please come closer."

As Clay looked down, the old man held the lamp over the sarcophagus. The flickering flame revealed an artfully painted coffin settled snugly inside. The elaborate gilded wooden lid was fashioned in the image of an ancient Egyptian.

"This is Lord Neskhons Nebit," the old man announced solemnly, "He was originally buried in a tomb in Leontopolis. In life, he was believed to have been a grand vizier of one of the pharaohs of the 23rd Dynasty."

"Cool!" the teenager exclaimed as he set his hands down to touch the top edge of a genuine Egyptian tomb. The rose-colored stone felt smooth as polished glass but cold. The high school student was curious. "Is there a real mummy inside?"

The professor smiled benignly. "*Oui*," he answered, "Though out of respect I prefer to keep it closed. Besides, too much light and exposure to moisture is not good for mummies. It tends to hasten rot and decomposition."

"I understand," the teenager replied, realizing that the mummy was probably priceless and had to be carefully preserved. The youth's eyes caught sight of four large stone jars with the heads of various animals nearby on a small wooden table. "Are those real canopic jars?" he asked.

The professor, moving closer with the lamp, shook his head. "*Oui*. They are the canopic jars of Lord Neskhons."

The young man appeared inquisitive. "These contain his heart and his guts?"

The professor smiled with mild amusement. "Well not quite, *mon jeune homme*," he responded. "The ancients believed that the heart was the Ka or soul, so it was always left inside the body. The four jars, however, do contain the viscera, which are the stomach, intestines, lungs, and liver. It was believed that the mummy would need those in the afterlife."

"Fascinating!" the young man answered, gesturing with his hand toward the stone sarcophagus, "I'm surprised that the Egyptian government allowed you to bring these wonderful objects out of the country."

Professor Delacroix's shoulders shrugged with seeming indifference. "Ah, these treasures left Egypt many years ago. Besides, I acquired many of my artifacts from other antiquarians and private collectors in the Middle East." The old man, walking back over to the sarcophagus, stretched out his withered hand to gently pet the coffin lid. "In any case, the people today in Egypt do not truly appreciate such exquisite treasures. Sadly, they are infidels. They do not venerate the gods and have forgotten the sacred spells and holy ceremonies to honor the deities and the Ka of their own ancestors."

Clay's eyebrows arched in surprise. "You actually worship the old gods like Ra, Horus, and Amun?"

The professor, his eyes radiating with emotion, smiled faintly. "Let me just say that while I am surrounded here by all of these relics of Ancient Egypt, I feel the presence of the people of the Two Lands and the immortal gods that they worshiped.

Clay rubbed his chin in thought. "I can't really blame you," he confessed with a twinge of envy. "If I worked here, I would feel the same way about the wonders and culture of Ancient Egypt."

The curator seemed genuinely touched. "I believe you would," he replied thoughtfully as he plucked his beardless chin.

Looking down at his cell phone, Clay realized how late it was getting. "I have to be heading home, sir," he replied, reaching out his hand, "but thank you so much for the tour. I'll try to come back again."

"*Oui.* I'm sure you will young man," the old man said with a slight bow as he extended his arm. Professor Delacroix shook hands with the teenager. The old man's hand felt rather cool and coarse. It was like gripping a dried-out corn husk.

With a curt wave, Clay turned around and departed. He had been at the museum longer than he had imagined. The sun was beginning to set, tinging the clouds a blood red. As he proceeded home down the street toward West 2nd, the teenager's mind pulsed with vivid images of what he had seen.

Disillusioned with his humdrum life, the young man blissfully fantasized as he walked. He fondly envisioned himself as an ancient Egyptian, riding a sleek chariot across the yellow desert sands or cruising on a royal barge down the cool waters of the Nile past the crouching sphinx and the Great Pyramids. But as he crossed Bridge Street, the daydreaming youth heard too late a harsh, screeching sound. Clay's head jerked around and his eyes froze in terror as a large Cadillac roared down on him before darkness engulfed him.

"*Mon jeune homme,* can you hear me?"

Clay moaned and shifted his head. As he twisted on an

uncomfortable bed, his arms and chest seemed unusually stiff. The eyelids fluttered and gradually opened. The teenager groggily looked up as if coming out of a long dream. It was fuzzy at first, but gradually his eyesight cleared and he found himself staring up at the lean form of Professor Louis Delacroix. The old man, lifting up an elegant ebony walking stick, tapped his red fez in salute.

"*Bonjour!* I cannot tell you how delighted I am to see you awake at last. You were in a terrible accident."

Clay nodded as he swallowed. His mouth felt parched and tasted of foul chemicals. "Yes," he replied weakly, "I remember now. I was on my way home from your museum and was crossing a road when I was hit by a car."

"Oui," the old man agreed, "It was in the Washington Daily News. Everyone was quite shocked, especially your classmates and family."

"I'm lucky I guess," he answered wearily, lifting up his arms to notice that they were still wrapped in bandages. "I could have been killed."

The professor grimly shook his head in profound disagreement. "My dear young lad, you *were* killed." he announced gravely. "I attended your funeral! It was quite touching to see so many mourners crowd into the Oakdale Cemetery to see you laid to rest. There was a big mound of beautiful red roses piled atop your grave."

The youth, as he lay on his back, was stunned and a bit confused by this strange and ridiculous pronouncement. Yet his face did not flush with anger or excitement. Indeed, his cheeks felt unusually cold. "What!" the teenager finally burst out, "That's nonsense! I am alive!"

"Well, you are now," the Professor replied, "Though it will take you some time to adjust to the reality of your new life."

It was only now that the teenager realized that he was not lying on a bed. Instead, he lay in what appeared to be a coffin. The insides of the wooden casket were neatly inscribed with rows of freshly engraved hieroglyphics. Shocked, the youth sat up and only now realized that his whole body was covered in linen wrappings. He looked around and found himself neither in his own home or a hospital but in what appeared to be the mummy room of the professor's museum.

There were lit braziers burning, and the smoky air was thick with the aroma of incense. As he glanced around he realized that he and the coffin he sat in were in a stone sarcophagus opposite that of Lord Neskhons.

"What's going on here?" he asked, his hollow voice trembling, as he stared down at his hands, which appeared pale and shrunken, "How can I have been dead and yet am alive?"

"*Mon jeune homme,*" Professor Delacroix replied, straightening his back, "You are now a mummy, but not an ordinary one. I discreetly stole your corpse from the funeral home and weighted the closed casket with stones. Returning your body to my museum, I have performed the ancient embalming process and through the incantation of sacred spells from the Book of the Dead, have just restored you to life."

"Me, a mummy!" Clay exclaimed with disbelief. "You're joking! I don't believe it!"

The professor gestured toward a table which had a lit clay oil lamp. In the flickering flames, the youth noticed four freshly chiseled stone jars, each topped with a different head, lined up behind the lamp.

"These are YOUR canopic jars," the elderly man replied in a sympathetic voice, "Open them up and look inside and then feel your chest. During the mummification process, I had to remove your internal organs. You will never have to eat or drink again. And note that you can both talk and smell but that you don't breathe."

His hands shaking, the teenager slowly lifted himself out of the sarcophagus. His fingers touched his wrists. There was no pulse. His hands thumped on his chest. It felt empty except for the rattling of a stilled heart. The youth walked over to a lit oil candle. He tried, but could not blow a wisp of wind from his mouth to extinguish the flame. Clay turned to the canopic jars. Lifting up the falcon-headed lid, he reluctantly peered inside. It was filled with intestines soaking in some sort of resin and smelling awful. He turned his face away in disgust and looked over to the old professor with a sorrowful expression.

"Oh my God, I AM a mummy!" Clay acknowledged with a slight shudder, covering his face with his hands. Though he tried to weep, he discovered that no tears came from his eyes. "I can't even cry. It's like I'm in my own horror film," he moaned.

"Do not worry, my son," the old gentleman reassured him,

placing his hand on the youth's shoulder. "There is no cause for despair. Your life will have no more of the illnesses and frailties that beset mortal humans. For you, there will be no more sunsets. You will live forever like the Immortal Osiris."

"How do you know that?" the teenager scoffed.

The old gentleman smiled. He pulled back, casually flung aside his red fez hat and pulled out an Egyptian head covering from his coat pocket. He set it on his head and raised his chin proudly.

"Because I am mummy! I am Lord Neskhons Nebit," he stated matter-of-factly as he twirled the end of his cane toward the other stone sarcophagus. "Only I was not a vizier in my other lifetime, but a High Priest of Osiris. My devoted followers performed the sacred spells over my body when I died of plague. I woke up and found myself alive once more but trapped in my casket buried in a vault deep underground. I lay there for over two thousand years until a French archaeologist in the service of Napoleon fortuitously unearthed my tomb, broke the seals and opened my coffin."

The old man sadly shook his head. "Poor man, he was the real Louis Delacroix. He was unhinged when he saw me and went insane. But I was finally freed to live my new life. I have moved about ever since. I have learned many languages and met many people. My travels eventually brought me to Washington, North Carolina.'

The mummified boy listened in silence. "Why did you do this to me?" he gasped.

The high priest of Osiris turned and picked up a linen head covering which was draped on the sides of the young man's coffin.

"Because you displayed a genuine affection and love for the culture and people of the Two Lands. Such people are rare to find in this so-called 'progressive'and 'modern' era. Your old life is in the past. Forget about your family and friends. You are dead to them. But you have a brilliant future ahead of you. You can assist me in running my museum. I will teach you the ancient ways and you will help me preserve the rich legacy of Lower and Upper Egypt. But we must not tell others what we are. Infidels are not yet ready for such knowledge." He handed the younger mummy the head covering which appeared newly sewn. "But what type of name is Clay? It sounds like another word for dirt. I think from now on we will call you Userkare," Lord Neskhons suggested. "It means 'The Soul of Re is strong.' A good name, I think."

The youth once known as Clay Cutler still reeled with the knowledge that his predictable old life was finished. He was sorely tempted to run away. "But to where?" he moaned to himself. "How could I go back home? How could I face my folks and family looking like this? Besides, the old mummy is right—I can't go back. For better or worse, this is my new life."

After some hesitation, the new mummy made up his mind. He slowly reached out his hand, snatched the head covering and placed it on his freshly shaved head. "Okay, but what am I to do?" Userkare asked. "People who knew me in my old life, my family and friends, will spot me if I ever go outside this building."

The elder mummy reached over and carefully adjusted the headdress on his young compatriot. "No need to worry, *mon jeune homme*. The mummification process took months to complete, during which time I moved my museum and its artifacts (including you) to a new location better suited than the damp and humid air of North Carolina. "

"Really?" Userkare responded. "Where are we?"

The old high priest walked over to a thick velvet curtain and pulled it open. Though it was past midnight, a flood of flashing light filled the room. The younger mummy stepped over to the window and found himself staring out on the majestic face of a huge sphinx with a gleaming pyramid in the background. Neon lights from nearby buildings and signs of a great city flashed continuously over and over.

"Sweet!" Userkare cried out with genuine delight. "We are in Las Vegas, right across from the Luxor Hotel!"

"*Oui*," replied Lord Neskhons. "The climate in Nevada is hot and dry—ideal for us. Damp air tends to promote mildew and moss." The old mummy smiled again and pulled out some casino tokens from his vest.

"Besides," he added, "who said that the life of a mummy has to be dull and boring?"

Author Biography

Lois Biggs Tetterton

Lois, a Pinetown, North Carolina, resident, attended Mars Hill College and graduated from East Carolina University. She taught school in Pitt County, Virginia Beach, Pinetown Elementary, and Bath High School.

A wife, mother, and bookkeeper for her husband's businesses, she has been married to Earl for 57 years. She has four adult children, seven grandchildren, two step-grandchildren, and one step-great-grandchild.

Lois has lived in the same house in Pinetown, built by Earl, for the past 50 years. She has no previous writing experience.

A Good Morning

By Lois Biggs Tetterton

"Heavenly Father, for your watch-care through the night, the blessings of a good night's rest, I thank you. Please guide my thoughts and actions through today, in everything I do, that I might honor you. In Jesus' name, A-men."

It's so welcoming—this warm and cozy kitchen. The coffee is already brewing, the ham in the griddle giving off its promise of good things to come. The reason for all this is right there—that big black beauty—my cast-iron wood-burning cookstove. Just a few years back, you would not find me so cheerful in the morning. You can see behind the stove where the open fireplace has been bricked in. Imagine trying to prepare breakfast, with one baby on my hip and another one on the way, stooped over that open fireplace. Don't let anyone tell you those were the good ole days. Believe me, anyone who's ever done it will tell you, the wood-burning cookstove is the way to go.

The preparations for our morning meal started last night. After washing the supper dishes, I sliced the ham, got it ready for cooking, fixed the coffee for brewing and then this morning, before going out to do his chores, our oldest son George got the fire in the cookstove going. He is such a smart little boy, but also always, a very hungry little boy. He doesn't mind doing this chore at all.

Looks like everything's going well, so I'd best quit lollygagging and get started on my job as chief biscuit maker. Over there on this small table, you can see my Granny Lizzy's wooden bread tray, a pitcher of clabber (maybe buttermilk to you), a stand of lard, and my personal favorite brand of flour, Snow Drop. But you ask, "Where are your measuring utensils?" I carry those with me wherever I go.

A two-hand scoop of flour will make a dozen biscuits, and since I have to fix four school lunch buckets, and since we are going to have lots of red-eye gravy for sopping, I should probably make about four dozen biscuits this morning. Next, I take three fingers, make a smaller scoop, and add the lard. A three-finger scoop is needed for each dozen—so, isn't that easy to remember? A two-hand scoop of flour and a three-finger scoop of lard equals one dozen biscuits. Put all of the flour in the middle of the bread tray, then in the middle of that, add the lard. All you do next is add clabber, a little at the time until everything is blended. How hard is that?

Wait a minute! I hear someone crying—sounds like James. He's been out feeding the chickens.

"Hey, Little Buddy. What's the matter?" ...... "That ole rooster tried to jump on you again? I'm so sorry. Remember, he thinks he's protecting his lady friends from something dangerous. He doesn't know you are bringing them their breakfast. Let's dry those tears. Hey, I've got a good idea. Wanna hear it? One day soon, let's wring that ole rascal's neck and have us a pot of chicken and pastry for supper." ...... "I thought you'd like that—like father like son, aren't you? Feeling better? Go on now and put on your school clothes; don't forget your homework. We'll be eating breakfast shortly."

"Liza, come set the table, please."

I'd best check the wood in the stove; it's impossible to make good biscuits without having a hot oven. Another piece of wood should do the job.

My method of getting this big lump of dough on a pan and in the oven is fairly simple: just pinch off a little dough, about the size of a pullet egg; roll it in your hands into a ball; plop it down on your biscuit pan and flatten it. Repeat forty-seven times.

While I'm doing this, let me share with you something I read in the *Ladies Home Journal*. The writer tells how the ladies in Charleston roll their dough out on a flat surface to about one-half inch thick. Then they take a little gadget that looks like a jar lid turned upside down, and cut out the biscuits, then place each one, perfectly cut the same, on their biscuit pan. Do they think that biscuits that look pretty has anything to do with how the biscuits taste? It seems to me some people have too much time on their hands.

Did you hear someone sneezing? That's Thomas. If you're looking for Thomas in the morning, just follow the sound of someone sneezing, and you'll find him. He's out in the barn, milking the cow. Let me get these biscuits in the oven and I'll go help him with the bucket of milk.

"That hay got to you again, huh?" ...... "Now Thomas, I know that hay bothers you, but you know we have to feed ole Betsy. You give her a bundle of hay, and she gives us this bucket of milk. I think that's a pretty good trade. Grab my handkerchief from my apron pocket and blow your nose.

"I've put a pan of warm water on the pump shelf on the back porch. Go wash your hands and face real good and then change into your school clothes. Maybe that will get rid of most of the pollen. Breakfast is almost ready.

"Elizabeth Marie, set the table. Now!"

Biscuits are looking good, coffee's ready, and I only need to make the red-eye gravy over here on the stove. Excuse me a minute. I need to run to the pantry.

I've got a dozen eggs to scramble, and I brought back this jar of pear preserves. These pears are so good on hot biscuits. Plus, I'll use some on biscuits for the lunch buckets.

This breakfast is fit for a king, or for three princes and one little princess. Time to call 'em in. It only takes this ole saucepan. Beat on it three times with this wooden spoon, and you'll hear them come running.

"Here come the cutest children in Walla Watt. All present and accounted for. Thomas, it's your turn to lead us in the blessing."

"A-B-C-D-E-F-G- Thank you God for feeding me. A-men."

"You all dig in—you need a full tummy to keep your brain working at school. I'll fix your lunch buckets while you eat.

"Liza, you've not brought me your lunch bucket." ...... "What do you mean you can't find it? I just bet if you go kick around some of those clothes on your bedroom floor, you'll find it.

"George, keep your elbows off the table, please. And son, slow down. There's plenty of food here, and nobody's going to take what's on your plate. Just look at you—there's pear preserves syrup dripping off your chin. Let me catch that with my apron.

"Here's the missing lunch bucket, thank you. It's pretty cold out there this morning. Pop said when he was leaving for work, he could smell snow in the air—whatever that means. I do think you should wear your big coats, gloves, and toboggans. And, if it's snowing when school dismisses, don't begin walking home. I'll hitch up the mule and cart and come pick you up." ...... "Glad you enjoyed it. It's time to get on the road. Go get your coats on."

These lunch buckets are prepared, each one with two ham biscuits and two pear preserves biscuits. Should be plenty for them until they get back home this afternoon. This cold weather calls for hot chocolate waiting for them. Maybe I'll have time to bake a batch of tea cakes, too.

"Mr. Thomas, just what do you think you're doing? You know the procedure here. You get a lunch bucket after I get a hug. I've put a couple of extra biscuits in your bucket to give to your friend, Joe John. I hear the stork made a delivery at his house yesterday— another boy. His mom may not have been able to fix him lunch today." ...... "You're welcome.

"Little Buddy, Did you do all your homework? What is six times four?" ...... "Try again." ...... "That's right. Let's get this jacket buttoned all the way to the top. Here you go." ...... "You're welcome."

"Sister, Pop and I are so proud of you for helping little Cassie with her reading. I just bet you're going to be a teacher one day. A lunch bucket for you." ...... "You are welcome.

"George, I think today would be a good day for you to give Lydia a break from your teasing. Be nice, okay? Anyway, I'm sure she knows you like her." ...... "You're welcome, and try real hard to be sweet.

"You children have a good day. Make your Mama proud. Boys, look out for your little sister. James, get out of that mud puddle!"

"Dear Lord, I'm giving these children back to you for a little while today. I know they are yours anyway, but please watch over them, protect them, and keep them safe. And, Lord, I can never understand why you have been so good to me. Thank you for all your love and blessings. In Jesus' name, A-men."

No, No, No! I feel a good cry coming on. Oh, well, at least I can cry and wash breakfast dishes at the same time.

Author Biography

Landis Wade

Landis Wade is a Charlotte author and trial lawyer who starts each day walking two rescue dogs named after characters from Larry McMurtry's classic western, *Lonesome Dove*.

He won the 2016 North Carolina State Bar short story contest for his story, *The Deliberation* and he's the author of *The Christmas Courtroom Adventure Series,* a set of whimsical legal mysteries where characters who believe in Santa Claus are put on trial and the time to Christmas is running out.

Landis serves as a Board member of the Charlotte Writers' Club and he is an active participant in CharlotteLit and the North Carolina Writers' Network. He's a 1979 graduate of Davidson College and a 1983 graduate of Wake Forest Law School.

When he doesn't have a dog leash or a keyboard in his hands, he's probably holding a fly rod, a golf club or a cold beverage at a Carolina Panthers or Charlotte Knights game.

Reflections Competition
Nonfiction First Place

The Cape Fear Debacle

By Landis Wade

I've often wondered what made my dad think that he and a friend could take four young boys on a trip down the Cape Fear River without much planning. I now have a theory.

It was the summer of 1969 and nothing seemed impossible. Astronaut Neil Armstrong had just taken one small step for himself and one giant leap for mankind, and Americans everywhere were imbued with a sense of adventure. About the time the lunar module *Eagle* landed on the moon in the Sea of Tranquility, the males of the Wade and Griffin households launched two boats on the Cape Fear River near Fayetteville, North Carolina. We would have been safer landing on the moon, but what did I know? I was only 11 years old.

In high school and college, my dad was a lifeguard at Wrightsville Beach. He was comfortable in, around, and on water. And that was the gist of the problem. He figured the Cape Fear was just another body of water. If he put a boat on the river in Fayetteville and pointed it toward Wilmington, what could go wrong? My point, exactly.

Dad loved to reminisce about the Cape Fear trip. Mom rolled her eyes every time the subject came up. It made sense. She was the one who had to come find us.

Did you know that tree limbs float in the Cape Fear? Neither did my dad.

Did you know that it's hard to camp along the Cape Fear? Surprised my dad, too.

Did you know there are locks and waterfalls on the Cape Fear between Fayetteville and Wilmington? Dad knew about this, but on cross-examination, he will admit he didn't know their precise locations.

Ever hear of *The African Queen*—Humphrey Bogart and Katharine Hepburn? Bogart played a character who swore it would be suicidal to try to navigate the Ulanga River in Tanzania, but he never had to go down the Cape Fear River with my dad. I suspect Hepburn would have given my dad a few tongue lashings on our trip.

Okay, I admit it. I was just a kid. I didn't think about the risks. My brother and his friend, Speedy, were 9-year-olds, and they didn't know any better, either. Speedy's brother was a year older than me, but none of us boys were worried. We didn't even flinch when one of our boats wouldn't start and the dads came up with Plan B. They said we could just throw the supplies into a small skiff and drag it all the way to the beach behind the boat that worked. It sounded good to us. Oh, and don't forget, we'd just landed a man on the moon, so the plan was solid.

When we arrived at the Fayetteville boat launch, the Cape Fear River had a sheen on top like melted milk chocolate. I wondered what lurked beneath the muddy surface—snakes, for sure. Probably worse than that. But it didn't matter. We didn't come to the Cape Fear to go for a swim. We came to be explorers.

Our plan was to go down the river, camp each night along the way, eventually pass the port in Wilmington, find our way to the Inland Waterway via Snow's Cut, and head back north to Wrightsville Beach where we would drop anchor and take our giant mankind steps ashore. We would land near my grandmother's beach cottage, where my mother and her friend awaited the return of their families, much like the wives of the Apollo 11 astronauts waited on their husbands to return from the moon.

The mothers had one job: drop the crew off in Fayetteville and take the boat trailers to Wrightsville Beach. And they did their part well. They put us on the river and waved us off from the dock. Then Mom walked to her station wagon, the one that sported the fake wood siding. I instinctively rubbed the wood on the side of the old Chris Craft dad borrowed from my uncle. It would be our home for the next three nights. Or so I thought.

About half a mile into the trip, we began to feel the bump of cresting waves caused by a steady breeze that blew up the river. The tree limbs that my dad didn't count on floated in the river, so the boys alternated as lookout on the closed bow of the boat. The bow had no rail. We just hung onto the center cleat. Appalled yet? Don't forget. This was 1969, before seatbelt laws for cars.

Ten minutes into the trip, we were alone. If civilization was out there, we couldn't see it, because our watery path was bracketed by thick tangled trees that bent over from the banks and touched the water. And there was not a boat in sight. Coming or going. We might as well have been on the moon.

When lunchtime came, we dined better than the lunar astronauts. Dad guided the old Chris Craft close enough to the river bank for us to toss a line over a tree branch and the boys climbed up. We ate peanut butter and jelly sandwiches, with our legs dangling over the Cape Fear River.

When we finished lunch, we took off, making slow but steady progress.

And then we smelled the smoke.

The smoke was courtesy of the dads' Plan B—pulling the skiff behind the Chris Craft. The skiff was fully loaded with tents, food and other supplies that should have been in a larger boat under its own power. The strain on the Chris Craft was too much. Our motor stopped. We floated in silence.

As we drifted around a bend in the river, the dads were hard at work trying to crank the engine. That was when the boys noticed that the river had changed in shape. Instead of a solid mass of water straight ahead of us, the water seemed to come to an end, next to a concrete structure. It only took us a few seconds to recognize this abnormality for what it was—a waterfall.

There are three locks and dams on the lower Cape Fear, providing over 110 miles of navigable water from Wilmington to Fayetteville. The first was finished in 1915 and goes by the unique name of "Lock and Dam No. 1." It's forty-three nautical miles above Wilmington, but we never saw it. Didn't even come close. Nor did we see the equally creatively named "Lock and Dam No 2," built near Elizabethtown in 1917. But we damn well saw number 3, which was built in 1935. It got a third-person name in 1965: "The William O. Huske Lock and Dam."

The ten-foot waterfall over Mr. Huske's dam, which was just to the side of Mr. Huske's lock, made a noise that got our attention. It was the sound rushing water makes when it pours over a ledge and splashes hard on rocks below. Kind of a rumbling sound, one you don't want to be caught near in a boat that doesn't work.

Modern-day maps, with fine print warnings drafted by lawyers, caution boaters about the waterfalls next to the three locks on the lower Cape Fear. One current map says that "swift currents can sweep you over the dam." No offense to the risk-adverse lawyers out there, but you didn't need to tell young boys such an obvious fact, even back in 1969.

The boys paddled hard with whatever they could find to move the Chris Craft and the skiff it was dragging to the side of the river without the waterfall. Seconds seemed like minutes as the sound of the waterfall grew louder and the cliff's ledge drew closer. The dads grabbed the tow rope and pulled the skiff to the back of the Chris Craft, lest it swing into faster water and pull us over the falls. The rest of us paddled for shore, with the bow of the Chris Craft pointed toward the outstretched arms of the riverbank trees.

When the Apollo 11 astronauts hurtled to the surface of the moon, alarms screamed in their capsule because they overshot their target by at least four miles. They missed dropping into large-mouthed craters that would have taken their lives, and with their fuel running low, they stuck their landing. We screamed a bit, too, dropped our bravado, and were no less fortunate to find a safe place to land.

The government-paid lockmaster stood on the concrete lock with his hands in his pockets as the Chris Craft bobbed in the water below him. He had a bemused expression on his face.

We must have looked like city dwellers, crammed into an overloaded boat, oblivious to the perils of the mighty Cape Fear River. At worst, he saw us as inexperienced fools. At best, he saw us as tourists with no idea how lucky we were to have made it this far and little notion of the slim chance we had to make it to the beach. Either way, he was one hundred percent correct.

As it turned out, we traveled no more than seventeen nautical miles from Fayetteville to the William O. Huske Lock and Dam. At that pace, it would have taken us at least five days to get to the beach. I'm pretty sure we had gas and food to last only three days.

After the lock filled with water, steel doors opened and we floated into a giant concrete shoe box. Once inside, the lockmaster pulled the plug and the water fell. When the large steel doors at the other end of the box opened, we saw more murky water. And more tangled trees that stood guard on each side of the river.

After we floated through the lock, my dad turned the ignition key and the motor came to life, bringing a shout of joy from the crew. The dads threw out the idea of adding more miles to the trip before camping for the night and the boys were all for it. The boat wasn't smoking, so the dads said, and we agreed, that the boat would be fine. As the old Chris Craft pulled away, I looked back. The lockmaster stood on the top of the lock. I saw him shake his head.

At this point in the story, you're probably wondering about the sanity of the dads. And with good reason. But five minutes after exiting the lock, the dads made an uncharacteristically smart decision. It happened soon after a drop of rain landed on the boat's windshield and the motor coughed. I looked up and saw thick, dark clouds over the edge of the tree line. The boat swung around. We headed back to the lock.

The lockmaster met us at the boat landing. My dad explained that we'd decided to camp at the lock for the night, a decision that made perfect sense. The William O. Huske Lock and Dam was a well-appointed recreation area with three acres of green space, picnic tables, and shelters. With the coming rain, we'd have a nice place to stay dry.

I noticed that the lockmaster had that same look on his face as he did when we'd pulled up to the lock the first time.

"You can't camp in the park," the lockmaster said. "Regulations."

I looked around. Other than the well-groomed government property that was off-limits, there was no other grass in sight. And certainly, no other shelters. In fact, there was not much of anything in sight except the lock, the waterfall, the river and the boat landing we stood on.

"Can't put your stuff on the boat landing, either." He was a man of few words, but piercing ones at that.

As it turned out, there was only one option. Across the river, where the rough water from the waterfall played out, we spied a sand and gravel beach about twenty feet long and ten feet wide. It was littered with broken tree limbs and sticks and was backed up by a hill full of thicket that was gradual at first and much steeper above. We decided to camp between the small beach and the steepest part of the hill.

We shuttled our tents and supplies across the river in the skiff and set up camp. We cooked a meal, played on the beach, and did some exploring, but it's hard to recall much of what happened next because my memories were drowned by the deluge that followed.

Water has a tendency to flow downhill and the universe made no exception that night. We found ourselves trying to sleep in a natural waterbed.

My dad had his own solution to the problem. He decided to fish and smoke his pipe, or so I thought.

He brought a fishing pole with him on the trip. Do you think he brought any bait or artificial lures? Of course not.

With a small hook on the end of his line and no bait, he went fishing and he did it while biting on a pipe that was too wet to draw fire from a match.

Bite. Cast. Reel.

Bite. Cast. Reel.

That was his prescription for the evening. He did it all night long.

The next morning, the sky broke clear, but the crew was a wet and beaten bunch. When we tried to start the motor on the Chris Craft, it was as dead as our spirits.

The lockmaster let Dad use the government's rotary phone, and he called the beach.

"What did he say when he called?" I asked my mother years later.

She couldn't recall his exact words. She just remembers the tone of the message:

"Houston, we've got a problem."

******

I drove to Fayetteville from Wrightsville Beach ten years ago on the highway that parallels the Cape Fear River and I saw a sign for the William O. Huske Lock and Dam. I couldn't resist.

I turned off the highway and drove to the end of a long dirt road. The gate was open, so I drove through and parked near the lock. When I got out and looked around, it was if I had exited a time machine calibrated for the year 1969.

Same concrete lock.

Same menacing waterfall.

Same pristine picnic area with covered shelters.

Same dark, mysterious river, flowing onward, after all this time.

I walked down to the boat landing and looked across the water. A remnant of our beach, worn by the river, was still there.

I thought about our adventure. The old Chris Craft. The skiff. The sandwiches in the tree. The waterfall. The lock. The beach. Night fishing. The rain. So much rain.

I sighed.

We didn't finish the trip, but we made it this far. Maybe that was enough.

I turned and headed back to my car.

******

A few months ago, my brother and I were cleaning out our parents' attic in advance of their move to a retirement community and we came across a tattered cardboard box full of eight-millimeter film canisters. On top of the stack was a covered reel with a masking tape label. The writing on the label said: "Cape Fear River, 1969."

Next to the box was the old Bell & Howell projector. Surely, it wouldn't work, after close to fifty years. But when we went downstairs and plugged it in, the light came on and the motor hummed. I snapped the reel on the projector and fed the tape through. A flickering miracle landed on the dining room wall.

"Dad, come quick. You have to see this."

For the next few minutes, Dad studied the grainy images on the wall, but he didn't say anything. I became worried.

In the previous six months, Dad had been struggling to recall names, dates, words, and sometimes, important events in the past. But this was the Cape Fear River trip. Surely, he'd never forget about that.

My brother and I watched Dad as he watched the movie. I glanced at the wall to see two young brothers with short blonde hair laughing in the back of an old Chris Craft. I saw a wake behind the boat, churning up muddy water. River banks streaming by. Boys climbing a tree. A man standing on top of a lock. A waterlogged tent. A small skiff.

My brother nudged me and I looked back at Dad. The clouds over his eyes were breaking up. And much like it did a half-century earlier, the sun came out.

Dad smiled a big smile. The kind I remember him smiling when he was on a boat. Out on the water. With the wind in his hair. When he was his happiest. When he was at his best with his boys.

And then he asked the question I'd been waiting to hear.

"You boys want to go finish that trip?"

Author Biography

Kate Ahearn

Kate Ahearn, pen name: Kate Louise Wood, lives with her husband in Edenton, North Carolina. A regular guest columnist for the Chowan Herald, she's had work published in the 2015 and 2017 editions of *Estuaries,* the visual arts and literary review of College of the Albemarle. You can read her blog at KathrynLouiseWoodAuthor.blogspot.com and visit her author Facebook page at WoodlyWords. She is a member of Hampton Roads Writers, North Carolina Writers' Network, and her local writers' group, Wordsmiths.

Reflections Competition
Nonfiction Second Place

Packing Her Bags

By Kate Louise Wood
(Kate Ahearn)

"When Mama moves to Wilson." That was our euphemism for when our mother would die and be buried beside our father in Maplewood Cemetery in Wilson, North Carolina. At ninety-two, and fighting ovarian cancer since the tender age of eighty-seven, Mama remained optimistic most of the time and continued to "fight the good fight" and demonstrate daily she did not intend to "go gentle into that good night." But...Mama was a practical woman, growing up in the Great Depression years, earning her college degree while our father dug foxholes on the bullet-ridden beach of Normandy, rearing two baby-boomers through the turbulent 1960's, providing home and care for her own mother during that matriarch's final years, then tending to our father as he struggled with heart disease and Alzheimer's before he "moved to Wilson." Life taught her that change was expected and death was inevitable— so one best prepare for it.

Mama was also a woman who liked to be in control. "Well, somebody better be!" was her unspoken but clearly heard message. Daddy was a gentle soul, more poet than a patriarch, who did his duty of providing for our family through the business world of commercial real estate, an occupation of his brain and work ethic but never of his heart and soul. His true world, the place in which his spirit dwelt, was in the nebulous realm of the wordsmith. In short, Daddy was that most pitiable creature, the frustrated writer. His natural inclination toward daydreaming and native aversion to the regimented world of business made for a difficult, albeit determined, career in management. Needless to say, this confusion in his psyche led to less than optimal stability in both his work and personal life. Enter, Mama. Command Central. The anchor of our family's boat when tossed upon Daddy's intermittently tempestuous seas. Such an anchor, it was not until I was middle-aged that I became aware of how close our family came, at times, to financial free fall when Daddy's artistic heart threatened to overrule his head. As much as I feel sorrow for my father's thwarted dreams, I am grateful for my mother's steely determination to keep our little vessel afloat, our household running smoothly, and setting Daddy back on course.

And so, practicality and control intact, Mama began packing her bags for Wilson. Part of the process was making sure she passed along as much of her wisdom as possible, mostly to me, her only daughter who, along with my understanding husband, provided her a place to live in those last years. In addition to the bedrock foundation of her legacy, that of unconditional loving faith in God and family, loyalty of friendship, kindness and connection with the four-legged among us, an abiding appreciation of nature, and the ability to laugh at one's own foibles, Mama made it her duty to try to impart knowledge to me in three basic areas: gardening, fashion, and home cooking. I do not use the word "try" loosely. Just as she was dead certain of her ideas in those matters, I was quite often, a hopeless (and, sometimes, adolescently stubborn) case.

First, gardening. Wherever Mama lived, she left a beautiful trail of flowers behind, and that trail stretched from Swansboro, North Carolina, to New York. Due to Daddy's mercurial career, we moved seven times in my first twelve years. Once I entered seventh grade, things settled down a bit and the next move did not occur until I was a freshman in college. Then, she and Daddy moved four more times before his funeral on September 11, 2001. Following his passing, Mama moved only twice more—to a senior citizen's apartment and then into our home. When she settled into her newly built bedroom suite, she announced she was not moving again until she moved to Wilson.

Whether it was an acre of park-like landscape or the confines of a balcony apartment, Mama not only set those little botanical beauties into the earth, she got down on her hands and knees in the sweltering heat of summer and did whatever it took to keep them growing and glowing. Alas, I have not inherited Mama's green thumb. In all honesty, it's not so much that I have a black thumb as it is I just don't have the requisite interest and motivation to move past the creative part of gardening I actually enjoy—the planning and planting—to the necessary part required to keep things alive. In other words, I'm a seeder, not a weeder.

Moving in with us presented Mama with both a golden opportunity—a largely untouched yard—and a challenge, actually two: her failing health and me. No longer physically able to get down and dirty with the plants, she had to rely on me to be her hands...and knees...and back. So, dutiful daughter that I was, I said, "Go for it! Be like Captain Picard and proclaim, 'Make it so,' and I will."

After a lengthy explanation of just who Captain Picard was and why he would make such statements, she smiled and said, "All right! I have been thinking about a few things we could plant." Well, of course she had. Not only did those things include a multitude of annuals and perennials, hanging baskets, and planters, there was a brick patio, fountain, and birdfeeder to be accessed from her backdoor. Mama maintained she was not the creative one in the family but her creativity bloomed and blossomed wherever she lived and put down roots. I know, in her mother-heart, she gave us a garden by which to remember her, but imagine my guilt when she moved to Wilson and weeds threatened to overtake her Garden of Eden!

Mama's second dose of wisdom centered on her impeccable fashion sense. Though never having had a sizable wardrobe allowance, she always chose her clothing with a taste for classic good looks. Not only was she a wiz at picking out lovely outfits that stood the test of time, she had necklaces, earrings, scarves, purses, shoes, and stockings to match them all. Her sock drawer overflowed with a rainbow of knee-high hose to correspond with every ensemble. She never left the house, whether for church or an oncology lab visit, without a fully put-together look including makeup and carefully combed and set hair, even though chemotherapy stole much of her baby fine locks.

As a rule, I think Mama's generation has always taken better care of their possessions than have successive ones and, in her case, this was especially true of her clothing. Coupled with her belief that one should never throw away anything still wearable, Mama accumulated enough clothing to outfit a small country. I assured her that donating to a charity thrift store was not the same as throwing her clothes away, but she remained doubtful. And, although her large, double closet was the object of much storage-envy by her visitors, it was still not spacious enough to hold everything. While organizing for her move to our home, I gently suggested that perhaps she didn't need so many skirts since she very seldom wore them anymore, preferring pantsuits and dresses. Her response? "Well, you never know. When I get older I may start wearing skirts again." After shutting the gaped mouth with which I presented my ninety-year-old mother, I just packed them up and loaded them into the car for their new home...the storage unit near our house, rented to hold everything her bulging closet could not.

Fashion was another area Mama found woefully absent in my lifestyle, my meager closet packed primarily with jeans and t-shirts. The youngest of four children, she was the first of her family to receive higher education, setting off for Louisburg College when she was sixteen and graduating from East Carolina University at twenty. Her degree in Home Economics Education set her on the path to teaching high school students and, later, attempting to teach her daughter how to sew. After all, when you cannot afford to buy fashionable clothes, you can always sew them yourself. Five decades later, I stood beside her as she lamented to the antique dealer, assessing the value of the lovely "Betsy McCall" doll she bought me when I was eight, that she'd gotten it in hopes I would learn to sew clothes for it but never did. Oh, my.

The third point of Mama's triangle of wisdom was that of home cooking, Southern home cooking to be exact. For her eighty-ninth birthday, I collected and published a slim but comprehensive volume of her recipes that became a treasured addition to the cookbook shelves of our family and friends. And, although I have not fully embraced the tradition of pork fat as the universal flavor enhancer, I can say I have successfully learned to prepare one staple of her cooking, something she always ate with seafood of any kind—fried lace cornbread. Yes! Not only have I learned to cook it to her exacting standards, I absolutely love to eat it. Fried cornbread is made of three simple ingredients producing a down-to-earth food that is simply delicious and connects me not only to my mother but to the generations of family cooks before her. Cornmeal, salt, and water stirred together and pan-fried in oil. That's all there is to it. But mixing the correct proportion of water to cornmeal and getting the oil to just the right temperature, is as much art and experience as it is culinary science. Cornmeal, salt, and water. Solidity, enrichment, and sustenance—three qualities of this home-cooked wonder that pretty much sum up my mother's contribution to our lives.

And so, on a summer Sunday morning, I sat beside Mama on a church pew, a place she longed to be each week but more and more was unable to make the physical effort required. Through much of the hour, she thumbed through a hymnal and matter-of-factly, with no sense of depression or self-pity, gently poked me and pointed out the hymns she wanted for her funeral service. Mama, ever practical, ever in control. If only I could control the tears welling up as I sang the next hymn in the church service. The minister must have surely thought he'd hit a nerve. No. It was just Mama, packing her bags for Wilson.

Author Biography

Pam Desloges

Pam grew up in the mountains of New Hampshire and spent much time on the rugged coast of Maine. After retiring from a small New England college, she lost interest in shoveling snow. She now lives in New Bern, North Carolina, with her husband, Max. She has been published in the anthology *Art Inspires Poetry*, the blog *Polly's Tea Kettle*, and a magazine for dog lovers, *Sniff & Barkens*. She is a member of the North Carolina Writers Network, the Pamlico Writer's Group, and is a founding member of the Neuse River Writers' Group.

Find her work at: https://www.facebook.com/pamdesloges

Using Margaret's Toothpaste

By Pamela Desloges

I found it in a bathroom drawer that hadn't been cleaned out. It could have been an oversight on his part, or maybe he had just given up at some point, and couldn't bring himself to deal anymore with her things.

Margaret died more than two years ago, losing her fight with pancreatic cancer. This is the house she had shared with Jim. Their grandchildren's pictures are on the walls and on the bookshelves, her linens on the beds, her dishware in the cabinets. She is everywhere in this house.

When Jim and I discussed living together, I assured him that she would not be forgotten. I understood that Margaret would always be here. He wept as he hugged me; he wasn't sure how to love us both.

Before I moved in, he had said, "It is your house now; do whatever you want. Make it your home." His two years as a bachelor showed up in every room—disorganized and messy. I tackled the pantry first, putting boxes on one side, cans on the other. Pasta with pasta, soup with soup, bird food with dog food, and soda with beer. He said, "You're nesting." And he smiled.

The day before I moved in, Jim asked if I wanted to use "her" bathroom for my own. I decided I would like that and started cleaning it out. One drawer was filled with empty photo frames, another with assorted magazines. The cupboard under the sink housed dog-shampoo bottles, an old hair dryer, and cleaning supplies. A few drawers were empty.

The contents of the bottom right-hand drawer caught me by surprise. It contained expired pain medicines, a syringe, nail clippers, curled prescription labels, and a half-used tube of toothpaste. I decided not to mention this drawer to him, and threw everything away, except the Crest. I tasted it and found that it was still good. *No need of wasting; I'll finish it.*

That night, I took it out of the drawer, twisted the cap off and squeezed.

I felt her for the first time.

"This is too much," I heard her say. *"I will share, but not this."*

I suddenly felt cold and lonely. My heart broke for her. There was so much I was already taking from her—this woman who had lost everything too early. The enormity of it hit me, in a six-ounce container. I gently put the cap back on, wrapped the tube in kleenex and placed it back in the drawer.

This is yours, Margaret. And I hoped she would forgive me.

Author Biography

Christina Ruotolo

Christina Ruotolo is a published author and freelance writer. She works in newspaper advertising, is a Hot Dish food writer, a bookseller at Barnes & Noble and an adjunct creative writing instructor at a community college.

She is the author of the poetry collection, *The Butterfly Net*, and co-author of the nonfiction book, *The Day The Earth Moved Haiti*. She has a BA in Communications and Literature and an M.A. in Creative Nonfiction from East Carolina University.

She has won writing awards through Wildacres Writers Retreat, Carrie McCray Awards for poetry, and has published poetry, nonfiction, and photography in past editions of *The Petigru Review*.

Reflections Competition
Poetry First Place

A Touch of Southern

By Christina Ruotolo

Aunt Madge was nearing eighty
when I was just ten
I remember her crouched low in her garden
the cabbage, collard, and mustard greens
swaying sturdy in afternoon light.
Her voice was rusty and worn-in like a silo
as she prayed to her plants
caressed leaves between liver-spotted hands
dug into the earth deep enough
to pull out all the answers.
She rubbed her tarnished fingers
round a rim of a Peach Snuff can
a wad of amber-colored tobacco
protruded from her leathery lip,
she spat a sticky warm line down
into a wide-mouthed mason jar.
The crow squawked a mid-day hymn
outside her white-clapboard house
in Piedmont North Carolina.
Rocking chairs pointed toward the sun,
tomatoes turning ripe with envy
the day making its way down low
as Aunt Madge rocked away sweat
snapping peas in an heirloom basket.

Author Biography

Consuelo Marshall

C. Inathe Marshall received an MFA in Creative Writing from California State University, Long Beach, in 2011.

She was poetry editor for *ARTLIFE Magazine* and her poems have appeared in *Convergence*, 2004; *ArtLife*, 24th Anniversary Issue, 2004; *Verdad Magazine*, 2009; *Spillway*, 2010; *RipRap*, 2011; *The Packinghouse Review*, 2012; *Beyond the Lyric Moment: Poetry Inspired by Workshops with David St. John*, 2014; *ELKE*, 2016; and *Redheaded Stepchild Magazine*.

She was the December 2016 Fairhope Center for the Writing Arts Writer-In-Residence and attended the 2017 Sewanee Writers' Conference.

Body Prints: Sonoma State University, 1970

To John Berger

By Consuelo Marshall

After the workmen left the library construction site,
we occupied it, lugging pints of white paint
and brushes. My roommate and I scurried
to the bathroom, cast off our clothes, painted
ourselves on both sides, just like buttering toast
for grilled cheese sandwiches.

When the coast was clear, we ran to the plywood
fence, pressed our warmth on its splintering surface,
first our front side then the back. Giggling, we ran
to the bathroom, splashed water haphazardly
on our breasts, pulling T-shirts over our heads.

In the morning, books in hand, we arrived
for our classes. My body prints had vanished,
like flocks of crows lifting from TV antennas.
My roommate's prints, shouting in sunlight,
spilled out to lolling couples on grassy knolls.

Looking back, I guess my roommate spilled
the beans to the guy I was dating. In darkness,
he came with claw hammer and crowbar, pried off
vandalized boards, heaved them in the back
of his pickup. I see him smile as he drove
the winding roads to Occidental.

It didn't take too many years for a builder
to find them at the dump, scratching his head
at those white figures; he used them to finish
off a bedroom wall in a Cotati house renovation
just one mile from the Inn of The Beginning.

Imagine the essence of my youthful body,
guardian all those years, behind sheetrock,
paint or wall flowers, awaiting an embrace
from plaster of Paris arms, glossed-over paper.

Reflections Competition
Poetry Honorable Mention

Fortieth High School Reunion

For Clayton Anderson

By Consuelo Marshall

I didn't want to see your junior high grin digging
a hole in space—it was you and me
in the supply closet with no light in seventh grade.
So pitch black, I could only imagine the glow
of peroxide in your bangs, the anger in your eyes,
shining like waves at the Wedge.

"Do you want to make out?" and before I could answer, light
bathed us, our angry teacher sending you
to the principal. You could get there blindfolded—
scuffing Sperry Topsiders on buffed concrete to his door,
sitting in a chair, its arms cradling the slump in your spine.

At the reunion, a raven-haired woman who had been popular,
riveted on photographs pinned on the easel,
turns as her eyes cloud with tears. I wanted to ask her about the
details: you living in the backyards of classmates, behind the pool
cabana where they found you,
cold and stiff.

"You aren't working to your potential," the principal told you, as
"The Duke of Earl" spun in your head, straight
from the dollar 45 on the turntable. What if you walked
in right now? Pushing me in a corner, asking me to make out? My
kisses would tell you we had something in common and it would
gather in strength, rise like
an uncatchable Southern California wave.

Author Biography

Dylan Fink

Hallo! I would like to introduce myself as Dylan Fink, an aspiring writer. One of my favorite pastimes is reading, and I always loved to do so. Books created a gateway for my own imagination to blossom into something more than just a simple thought. With my imagination, I could create mass expanses of terrain, huge worlds where people of all types could live. Deep space battles, magical beings, gods fighting over the planet. I want to inspire other people to use their imagination in writing and in reading. That is my goal in writing, and I hope you enjoy.

Coward

By Dylan Fink

8 years from now: College Graduation
13 years from now: Invent Chemical Cure for Mustard Gas
15 years from now: Holographic Training used to Train Soldiers
18 years from now: World War Three begins—USA, Britain, France, Japan, Germany vs. Russia, North Korea, China, Vietnam, Cuba
20 years from now: Our short story begins.

It's quite a few years since my childhood. I don't like being an adult. I'm not allowed to use my creativity, as I'm supposed to be "mature." I'm 34 years old and I'm not married, nor ever had a girlfriend. World War Three is happening, and I refuse to do anything about it.

Catherine... I'm sorry.

Being a World Renowned Chemical Engineer means that generals of all armies want me to help them. They ask for mechs, they ask for chemicals, they ask for cures... but every time I refuse to help them. War isn't my strong suit, and I hate the fact that people have to go to war over silly things and use others to fuel the silly battle. I would feel like an associate to murder if I helped. It just isn't right.

Why did I stop talking to you? Why did we stop talking?

I invented a cure to stop the infection mustard gas causes. I created holographic training procedures. I even made a modern-day Archimedes Death Ray. But I refused to help any further. I couldn't help any further. My own morals would have gotten the better of me. All these things I wanted as a child, all these dreams I had, put to use in a battle of countries.

Why did you have to move?

I wish I could be a child again. I wish I could imagine these death machines rather than have them real. I wish people didn't fight. I wish people were nice to each other, that everyone got along.

Is it because of your heritage? Of family pressure?

But that's never going to happen. People are naturally evil, naturally selfish, and only through teachings can they have morals, have manners, be nice.

I'm sorry. I need you again. Please speak to me.

It's no wonder we started the war. Not Russia, but America. The normally neutral country started World War Three. But it really was no wonder we did. Russia had stationed many, many boats off the border of Canada, seemingly preparing for some form of a battle. Canada itself was on edge from this maneuver—it hasn't had too many good events with Russia—and was hoping that they wouldn't attack them. Not only that, but Chinese and Vietnamese forces were gathering on the edge of the sea, near Japan. America wasn't having any of it and took the first initiative to attack. They sent a few battleships towards the Russian boats near Canada, and fired upon them. This one battle, known as "77-я дивизия дивизии," which translates to "The 77th Division Siege," sparked a fire in everyone that led to World War Three.

I hope you're okay. Please be okay. Please come back to me.

When I look in a mirror, all I see is a coward. Someone who doesn't look out for himself, someone who can't hold his own in a fight. Someone who's too scared to do anything without someone else's help. Others may see me as a kind individual who doesn't want war, who advocates peace, but all I see is a coward too scared to live up to the fact that people are naturally evil, and will go to war no matter what you do.

Please speak to me again. I....

I never...never spoke to her again. I never gained the confidence to do so. She was the nicest girl I've met...I wish I'd asked her out. I wish I had the courage. I wish I wasn't a coward. I wish...I wish I could reverse time and stop me from never talking to her.

I need you now, more than ever. Catherine...

Why am I so dumb? Why did I have to piss her off? Why did I have to say those things?

Why... Why....

Why did I leave you when you needed me?

I was simply walking to work, avoiding all eyes. I never was the most popular kid, not to mention adult. Even as a World Renowned Scientist. Most people kept their gaze to themselves, not caring about what I do with my time. It can be seen as sad, but I don't mind. I'm used to it. I'm used to neglect. Anyway, I was walking to work and stopped at a coffee shop.

Ordered a latte, sat down, and watched the news. And, as it has been for the past two years, they were talking about the war. I didn't need more reminder that I'm not helping, so I started to get up and leave. As I started to leave, the news anchor said, "Switzerland has been Russia's new target of attack, as the city of Geneva has fallen completely to Russian control in just 3 days." I stopped dead in my tracks.

Geneva? I thought. *That city's important, isn't it? Didn't one of my friends move there? Nathan? No, he's still in the U.S. John? He's in Florida, isn't he? Then who was it...* Then it hit me. The one person I lost contact with. The one girl I wanted to stay with me. The girl who may now be dead, and I couldn't say goodbye.

Catherine.

I ran out of the coffee shop, panicked. What if she died? I haven't spoken to her in years, but I'm still worried about her. I wanted to text her, I still had her number, but would it be weird after all this time? Would she even remember who I was? God, I made so many mistakes in my past, I wish I could make those up, I wish I could travel through time.

I wished so many things, but I didn't have time to think about that now. Not only was I nearly late to work that day, I did not get much done, I spent the entire night worrying that the person who was once my closest friend was gone forever without one word of goodbye. The next day, I was off, thankfully, but she was still on my mind. I couldn't get her out. No matter what I did, I was always thinking of her. I barely ate, barely slept, and my friends were worried sick about me. They thought I was going through a midlife crisis, a depressive phase. But I wasn't, not entirely at least.

I followed the news closely, seeing how the war effort was going. Many Geneva citizens were interviewed, not one was Catherine. "It was a massacre," one said. Another spoke about

Russian forces. "There was tank after tank, soldier after soldier. It was relentless, it felt like there was no end to the attack." I was tempted to help take Geneva back if only to see if she was okay. In the back of my mind, I had the lingering worry of her death, but I tried to push it off as much as I could.

About a week after I first found out about Geneva, one of my friends who was out surveying the damage in Geneva, told me that, "The Russians didn't just take over the city, they demolished it. Most buildings are burnt to the ground, only a few were left standing, and those that were are mostly destroyed and uninhabitable."

That only increased my worry. What if she survived, but is living in the wreckage of her old home?

It was three weeks before I got the text.

I was walking in the park, the one place I can go for solitude. It was peaceful, the only living things around were trees and animals. No human distractions disturbed me. I ended up sitting on a bench and took out a paper and pencil, and started writing, as I usually do when out there. Then my pocket buzzed. I thought nothing of it at first, probably a random notification on my phone. Then it buzzed again. And continued buzzing for a while. Then stopped. Then another quick buzz. I was getting annoyed at this, so I was going to set my phone to mute. I pulled out my phone, turned it on and... saw that Catherine had texted me.

"Hey. I know we haven't talked in a while, but I need your help, really badly. I'm gonna make this short, I can tell you it all later, but I need a place to stay for the next few weeks, months, or even years. I know you probably hate me by this point, but please. For old times' sake?

"Please Dylan. I need you. I don't care about the past, and you shouldn't either. Please forgive me for what I did. I forgive you, and I need you again. Please."

I didn't know what to say at this point. She was alive and needed my help. And she forgives me.... I never would've forgiven myself for what I did and said...

I replied, "178, Morgie Lane, second floor, third room, in case you forgot. You can stay as long as you want. Just don't break anything, don't be too loud, and, for the love of god, don't steal all the food. I need to eat too."

It took her awhile to respond. I guess she was flustered by this too. "Nothing I say will thank you enough, so I hope this is good for now. Thank you, so much."

"You're welcome."

After I sent that last text, I was ecstatic. She was alive! And she actually wanted to talk to me again. I wanted to jump up and down, run around like a kid. Then I remembered that I was in public. Why does society have to make that taboo?

I spent the rest of that day in the park, just thinking about life. When I walked back to my apartment that day, my landlord, Gilmore, noticed I was a lot happier than usual.

"Dylan, my friend, how are you? You seem more jovial than usual!"

"I'm fine," I replied. "Got a text from Catherine. She's staying with me for a while." "Catherine is returning? My, she was a sweetheart. It'll be nice to see her again!" "Yes, it will. Make sure she gets a fair welcome if I'm out."

"That I will do, my friend. Have a good rest."

"You too." I started up the stairs and entered my room. It felt nicer to be there, knowing Catherine was coming back. I spent the rest of that night thinking about her while eating, and as I drifted off to sleep, I remembered how good a life I'd had with her, and how many mistakes I'd made in my life. But that was in the past, and this was a time to set my life in a different direction.

"It takes courage to grow up and become who you really are."

-E. E. Cummings

"Courage is being scared to death and saddling up anyway."

-John Wayne

"Dear past,
Thank you for all the lessons.
Dear future, I am ready."

Author Biography

Elizabeth White

I have always been interested in the arts. My interests have evolved from drawing to expressing myself in poetry, but I've always found comfort in creativity.

I got into poetry about and a half years ago. In a way, it brought me back to life in a time when I was not doing well.

I intend to collect all the poetry I've written and put it in a book and hopefully publish it.

Reflections Competition
High School Poetry First Place

I See Home

By Elizabeth White

Twenty years to home, where the sun glows
And a light touch could make the whole morning a blur.
I still have everything, but, "Mama knows...."
Or, well, she knew, but we aren't all as wise as we believe.
The silence is bliss with you by my side,
Your rhythm becomes the music and there's my sanity, washed up
on shore.
And all because I just wouldn't, or perhaps couldn't, abide...
I swore I would fight ruthlessly to protect what I hold dear.
It was a civil war, but fight I did.
With all the love and happiness I am blessed with now,
You can't tell me my opposers aren't still winded.
I found a place out in the mist, where I fit.
This old home creaks and talks,
Tells me not to be afraid and "Don't you ever quit."
Sometimes it gets bleary when I imagine it, but twenty years from
now I see home.

I *always* see home.

Wrapping Up the Reflections Competition

The Reflections Competition blind juried format contains two important changes from prior competitions.

In the past, Pamlico Writers. Group Board of Directors members were not allowed to participate in the blind competitions in the belief that their close tie with the organization offered an appearance that tainted the competition if a board member won an award. The board realized that talented writers have been denied an opportunity to participate.

Starting with the Reflections Competition, board members were allowed to participate with the proviso that should a board member win an award, that win would be vacated but the member's work would be included in the published anthology. To facilitate this, jurors were instructed to choose the normal first, second, and honorable mention awards plus two alternates. Board member Doris Schneider won an award in the Fiction Category. Her entry follows.

The second change involves revealing juror identities. The thought was that revealing the identity of jurors might lead them to situations in which authors might attempt to compromise their decision. In the Reflections Competition, juror identities have been revealed and their chosen work is published below as part payment for their services.

Author Biography

Doris Schneider

Doris was born in Texas and lived all over the U.S. and Canada. After 33 years of teaching theatre at William Carey University in Hattiesburg, Mississippi and North Carolina Central University in Durham, Doris retired to little Washington where she paints, designs jewelry, plays the violin and writes.

Doris has published two novels, *Borrowed Things* and *By Way of Water,* and has short stories in the anthology, *A Carolina Christmas.* She is currently seeking publication for her novella, *Drummer Girl.*

Her time is divided between the North Carolina coast and the mountains, where her husband Jim Coke raises wildflowers.

The Truck

By Doris Schneider, Pamlico Writers' Group Board Member

Ping! Joey ducks...Ping! More shots fly past his ear.... Searching for another place to hide, he quietly steps up on the running board and crouches, slowly rotating his head up and looking in the side mirror. Because the mirror is tilted up, he sees nothing but the reflection of the high gray inside of the ancient barn. He carefully reaches up and angles the mirror down...just a little...just...enough...to see....*the pitch–fork! behind him!...*just...as a hand...***grabs him!!!***

"Ahhhhhhhhhhhh!!!!!!!" Joey screams as he tries to run. Nathan rises up from inside a barrel, his eyes as big as saucers.

But Joey can't get away. It's holding his shirt.

"Joe!" it says—in a soft familiar voice. "Hold on, Buddy." He stops trying to run and sheepishly turns to face...Grandma. Nathan is laughing so hard, he tips the barrel over. It lands on hay with a soft whoosh—no damage to barrel or boy.

"What have I told you two about throwing rocks?" She crosses to the truck and examines the side for dents.

"They were just little ones," Nathan whines as he crawls out of the barrel. Then he laughs again. "You should have seen your face, Joey."

Still shaken from his fright, but trying not to show it, Joey drops nonchalantly to a bale of hay. Nathan joins him, still teasing.

"I see a scratch!" she announces, then turns to glare at the two offenders, eyebrows raised and wrinkled lips pursed, as she tries to look stern. But Grandpa's overalls are so baggy on her, she just looks funny. The boys bite their lower lips, trying unsuccessfully to hold back a smile.

"What's so funny about a scratch?" she demands.

Nathan, younger but by nature bolder than Joey, says, "How can you see a scratch, Grandma? That old truck is so beat-up and dirty...and it has all that green stuff on it."

She gives up on being tough and laughs with them while she finds an empty five-gallon paint bucket, places it upside down between the boys, and sits. "That's moss. I guess the moss on that truck is like the gray in my hair. It says we're old, but it's also kind of beautiful. I assume you've noticed how beautiful my gray hair is." The boys giggle and lean against the woman who has always been their champion.

"Have you ever looked real close at moss? It's like a perfect tiny world. From a distance, it just looks green, but up close it has lots of colors and shapes. It can loosen your imagination."

"Up close, your hair has lots of colors too, Grandma," Nathan says, with a bit of surprise.

"You want me to wash it, Grandma?" Joey asks.

"The moss or her hair?" Nathan teases.

"The truck!"

"Nope," she admonishes. "There's a hen nesting under it— unless you two scared her away. Besides, I kinda like the way it looks." She leans forward, her elbows on her knees and her head resting on her hands. "But there was a time when she was 'cherry.'"

"What's 'cherry' mean?"

"It means she was perfect. Your Grandpa made her shine. He was so proud." She smiles and allows her mind to drift.

Joey and Nathan roll their eyes at each other. Nathan starts to get up, but Grandma pulls him back down.

"How much do you boys know about your Grandpa?"

"Everything," Joey responds. "He grew up on this farm. His Daddy grew up here, too. And our Daddy grew up here."

"Yes," she sighs, "But it's not how they made their livings. The grain raised on the farm fed the animals and the garden gave us vegetables and seed money, some to sell and some to keep. But it wasn't enough to keep us in basics."

Nathan looks suspiciously at her, knowing that she can be forgetful and that she can be a tease. "What was his job?"

"Oh, he did lots of things. In those days, you developed many skills just to keep things together on a farm. One time he worked as a mechanic. For a while he delivered milk. But construction was his best paying job, and he liked it. He liked working outside with his hands."

Still unconvinced, he asked, "If Grandpa had a job, who took care of the farm?"

"I did, Nate, and your Daddy helped when he wasn't in school. He was driving vegetables to market in that same truck when he was no older than you, Joe."

Joey's mouth flies open. "He was driving a truck when he was ten?"

"Well, maybe eleven. But he looked fifteen. When he was seven, like you Nate, he worked in the fields, right beside me."

"He shoulda called 911!" Nathan mumbles in half disbelief.

"And what, get me arrested for child abuse? There wasn't a 911 then. And all the children on farms worked after school. The ones in town had paper routes or bagged groceries or something. They didn't have Game Boys or their own cell phones. We didn't even have a television."

"So, when did Grandpa buy the truck?" Joey asks as he gets up and stands on the running board, peering through the dirty window at the gear shift, trying to imagine driving it.

"He didn't. His Daddy bought it after he sold some of our land that was closest to town. It was pretty land with lots of trees, but no good for farming. He was sorry afterwards. They cut all the trees and built ugly houses.

"But it was enough money to put a new roof on the house and buy that truck and still put a little away for emergencies. When Papa Joe, your great-grandfather died, the truck became your Grandpa's."

Joey jumps down and sits at her feet. She ruffles his hair.

"How old was Grandpa?"

"He was twenty-four, just home from the war. Papa Joe died while Grandpa was in Korea."

Knowing the answer, Joey asks anyway, "Is that when you met Grandpa?"

Her eyes glaze over as the memories rush past. She hesitates before surprising them with a story they don't know. "He drove up to my place of employment."

"You had a job?"

"That's right. I was a carhop at the Wagon Wheel Restaurant."

"A what?" Nathan asks.

"A carhop. In those days people could drive their cars up to what we called a drive-in restaurant, and a girl would come out and take their order and then bring it out to them when it was ready."

"Isn't that the same as a drive-through?"

"Oh, no! The cars were parked, and music played loud enough for everyone to hear. The car windows were all rolled down and we had trays that fit on the door. People sat right there in their cars and ate their food, which was served to them by carhops—like me, wearing roller skates."

The boys laugh but stop when she looks at them. Joey soberly adds, "Very cool, Grandma."

"Teenagers would come to get milkshakes and hamburgers. They showed off their cars and flirted with each other."

Nathan scowls, but Joey betrays an interest. "I think I saw something like that in an old movie."

"No doubt. Anyway, he drove up one night in a dusty truck, and another girl waited on him. But every time I walked past, I could feel him watching me. He was older and bigger than the rest of the boys that hung out at the Wagon Wheel. He made me nervous."

"Sorry Grandma," Nathan laughs, "but I can't even imagine you nervous. How old were you?"

"I was seventeen. Anyway, he came back the next night and parked where I'd have to wait on him. He sat there all night, drinking one milkshake after another. And his truck had been washed until it shined.

"One of the girls told me that she knew his family and that his daddy had recently died. That changed everything. I understood then why he just sat so quiet and stared. Maybe he wasn't even starin' at me. He was just sad. ...Anyway, he asked if I had a boyfriend. I said, 'not anymore.' He asked to drive me home, and I agreed. My feet and legs were so tired from skating that I could hardly stand.

"As we were driving away, something hit the back window and cracked it. Dan slammed on the brakes, got out of the truck, and walked to the alley by the restaurant. He disappeared into the dark, and I was scared to death, not for me because I know this town. I was scared for him...or maybe for whoever he was after. I got out and looked in the back of the truck. There was a rock—not a big one, but big enough. It wasn't much bigger than what you two were throwing."

Finally, she has her grandsons' rapt attention. "It seemed like a long time before I heard footsteps. Dan and someone else were walking to the truck. When they got closer, I recognized my last boyfriend, Bobby Sloan. They walked up, and nobody said anything. Dan cleared his throat like he was waiting. I think you know what I mean."

Both boys nod, well aware of their grandfather's ability to shame without words. "Bobby couldn't look me in the eye, but he sort of mumbled an apology for disturbing my evening. Then he apologized to Dan for breaking his window. Dan still didn't say anything—just waited. Finally, Bobby said he'd pay to have the window fixed. Dan held out his hand. Bobby shook it, looking like he was going to pee in his pants. And then he left."

Her grandsons hoot at the image while she rises, dusting off her overalls. Knowing her story is over, they jump up and go to the truck, checking the back window. "It's still cracked," Nate announces.

"Wait a minute," Joey says. "Is Bobby Sloan the same as Robert Sloan—Grandpa's best friend?"

"Yep. And the crack that's there now happened later...another story for another time."

"Come on, Grandma, tell us another now."

She smiles and steps to the truck bed, peering into the moss growing here and there. "Look close...real close. Loosen your imagination and feel yourselves inside it—a new and different world, full of green and bounty."

The boys do as bid, their eyes close to the moss, waiting to be enchanted.

"Their world seemed perfect to the King and Queen of Mossland," she whispers.

"Aw, Grandma," they chime together.

"Remember, loosen your imagination. After the royal wedding, the Queen quit her job as a carhop, and the King provided milk for his kingdom, delivering it himself. He had to rise at three o'clock in the morning, but he was finished by noon and could help his Queen in the fields, where they grew food for the kingdom. In a short time, the Prince was born. He surprised his royal parents by turning out to be a superhero, a Transformer." The boys giggle.

"He was a student in the mornings, and then morphed into a farmer in the afternoons, stronger and taller than any of the other boys, and able to drive their produce to market in the royal truck. But he was lonely. So he asked for a little sister. His parents agreed and soon a Princess was born."

At the mention of a girl, the boys lose interest, but she continues, "Everyone in the kingdom rejoiced, and it seemed that the Princess was a superhero also. Her eyes were as blue as the sky, and her hair as fair and soft as the clouds. One day, when she was still a toddler, she morphed into a dove and flew up so high, she entered a different kingdom. The air was different there, and after she learned to breathe it, she could never return to her Mossland. The King and Queen, and even the Prince missed her. But she sent a messenger to ease their sorrow, and they eventually understood that she was needed in that other world."

"Grandma," Nathan laughs, "do we look like babies? That was just a fairy tale."

"Oh, sorry, I forgot how grown you two are. Go wash up for supper. But come back here after and pick up your rocks. I don't want to step on one and get a stone bruise."

Joey pauses, looks at his grandmother, and for only a moment holds eye contact. She wonders if someone has told him more of the fairy tale. Then he smiles brightly and turns to Nathan.

They run off, laughing and shoving, the nearest thing to endearment between brothers.

Millie sits on the bucket again, staring at the truck. She thinks on all the times Dan took her home after work, the feel of his large hands rubbing her sore feet when they parked down by the river; the way his eyes gradually lost that haunted look; the joy they each felt in the other's company, in the other's touch.

She remembers their wedding, so simple compared to weddings today. Her mother served cake and punch in the church basement after the ceremony. And their honeymoon was just a weekend alone in his father's empty house. It was all they needed.

Millie remembers Dan driving her to the hospital when Johnny was about to be born; how she bounced on the hard seat and cursed the truck for its rough ride; how slowly and carefully Dan had driven home again with his wife and infant son beside him.

She rises, laughing silently, remembering their son Johnny learning how to drive and landing in the ditch as he tried to back down the long driveway. Walking to the front of the truck, she looks at the big dent in the fender and remembers a shamefaced Johnny telling his dad that he had run into a telephone pole, missing a sharp turn while driving too fast on an icy road.

And then she looks down at the flat tires—all four of them—all flattened by the same pitchfork that had frightened Joey. She grimly remembers that time when Dan turned away from her, overwhelmed by the loss of their second child, a daughter whose name she still cannot speak, how he blocked out grief with alcohol.

One night, after running out of whiskey, he grabbed his keys to go for more. She tried to stop him, and they fought, slapping and shoving, then punching—while their fourteen-year-old son watched. Then Johnny ran out of the house, and Dan followed after knocking Millie down. He found Johnny with the pitchfork. His son had stopped him from leaving, and the punctured tires were never repaired or replaced.

Dan sobered up and left the old truck the way it was as a reminder. After days of working in the fields, sweating out the alcohol, and mumbling to himself what his wife hoped were prayers, he walked to town. He went to the bank and then to Robert Sloan's used car lot, and bought another truck.

Millie moves to the passenger side and looks through the window, trying to imagine the young girl and her soldier, trying to recapture her youth...and Dan's. She sighs, knowing it's gone, and knowing she wouldn't relive it—not because it was bad, but because...it was enough.

It was enough because of the dove. One day after Dan had sobered, and their life had returned to its sad routine, a dove flew into the yard and lighted on a branch outside the kitchen window. Doves were not uncommon in the state but had never been seen on their land. Another dove joined her, and together they built a nest on that same tree branch where Millie and Dan and Johnny could watch her sitting on her eggs, and then later...feeding her downy babies. Now there are many doves in the surrounding trees that come and go with the seasons, and there are "No Hunting" signs posted around the periphery of their land.

"Yes," she sighs with an image of the first white bird looking through the window as if she had flown home, "it has been enough."

Bending over, she looks under the running board and sees the hen, still on her nest. "Take your time, Darlin'," she whispers. "This old truck's not going anywhere."

Millie pats the fender, then turns to the house, calling to her Dan—her soldier, her lover, and her friend. He's in the vegetable garden, weeding. He weeds because he knows it's a task she hates. When he looks up, she smiles, waves, and calls him to supper.

Author Biography

Marni Graff

Marni Graff is the award-winning author of *The Nora Tierney Mysteries*, set in England, and *The Trudy Genova Manhattan Mysteries*. She writes crime book reviews on her website at www.auntiemwrites.com.

She is Managing Editor of Bridle Path Press, and a member of Sisters in Crime and the North Carolina Writers' Network. All books available in paperback, Kindle and Audible at Amazon and Bridle Path Press.

Email Marni at bluevirgin.graff@gmail.com

Reflections Competition
Fiction Juror

Harkers Island

By Marni Graff

Crossing berm and strand, serene
Above our earthly turmoil,
The horses run unbridled in playful gambado
Along the sandy shore.
Frothy graybeards leave their swashmarks,
Crossed by hooves of cantering joy.
Tall reeds stand guard in the dunes,
Alert to the horses' freedom.
The sun's light dances off their shiny hides,
Reminding us how it feels
To walk barefoot in the sand.

River Morning

By Marni Graff

Flat brown water ripples
Rhythmically against the bulkhead.
The susurration of a breeze
Through dry yellow marsh grass
Brings a blue heron to the shore.
Huge gray wings flap;
With a shriek
He takes to the air,
Circling overhead, thin legs dangling,
Searching for breakfast.

Across the creek
Dogs yap sharply in cadence,
Training in the woods for the hunt.
A loon's call echoes,
Repeated back
By the dog-like bark
Of a wide-winged tundra swan.

Two scarlet cardinals in a pine tree
Sing the day awake
Courting a dun-colored female,
Who flirtatiously darts and lands
On the copper roof, preening.

Three tall purple martin houses
Stand erect
Waiting for sentinels to guide
Their flocks and fill them with
Chattering families along the
river's edge.

At Angus' grave,
Yellow crocus and paperwhites
Thrust their heads through
Clay earth,
Bringing spring and memories of
A dog who loved
This river and swam it daily
To chase wood ducks and gulls away.

Author Biography

Richard Knowles

Richard Knowles began writing after retiring, about six years ago. Since then he has been a winner in a number of writing contests. He is a two-time winner in both the Pamlico Writing Contest and the Carteret Writers Contest. This year he was also a winner in the Porter Fleming Literary Competition, sponsored by the Morris Museum of Art in Augusta, Georgia. Richard's favorite genres are nonfiction and fiction. He currently resides and writes on Harkers Island with his wife, Jill, and labradoodle, Rosie.

Reflections Competition
Nonfiction Juror

The Temple Bench

By Richard Knowles

The clear midsummer sky and crisp, dry air held the promise of a pretty day in the mountains of Japan. The twenty-minute ride on the commuter train, from the village of Shinonoi to Nagano, took us along the Chikuma River, past fruit orchards and small Japanese gardens. On the way up the broad, fertile valley, the train made brief stops at three other small, rural villages to pick up passengers headed into Nagano. Mostly teens, they were on their way into the city to spend their Saturday in the glitzy department stores and noisy video gaming arcades. Along the way we passed farmers, usually husbands and wives, working in their fruit orchards and vegetable gardens, much like their ancestors had for centuries in this valley. The valley's serenity and ancient rural charm stood in stark contrast to the tall buildings, bright lights, and fast living of Nagano. For the young people on this train, the idea of toiling and sweating in the family garden could not compete with the lure of the big city just ahead. I too was drawn to the big city this day, but for a different reason.

I had been in Nagano for about six months, part of a computer technology team working on the upcoming Winter Olympic Games. Nagano, Japan was the host city for the XVIII Olympiad, to be held in February of the following year, 1998. The tiny village of Shinonoi housed the technology team's work facility, and that was where I lived; I wanted to spend my year in Japan immersed in Japanese culture. Everybody else in my group either rented an apartment in Nagano or stayed in hotels, flying back and forth to the United States every couple of weeks.

My destination that morning was Zen Koji Temple, a 7th Century Buddhist temple that sat on a hill at the north end of the city. The temple came first; the city grew up at its feet. Zen Koji was the cultural centerpiece of this part of Japan, a pilgrimage destination, as it had been for over a thousand years.

On my way from the train station to the temple, I needed to stop at a bakery. When in Nagano several days ago, I accidentally left my wallet on top of an ATM near the bakery. A day later, after disassembling the entire contents of my apartment, and checking every bag and pocket multiple times, I had given up on finding the wallet. The next morning a Japanese coworker came to me with a message he had gotten from a bakery in Nagano. Somebody had brought my wallet into the bakery and asked if they could help him find the owner. It was obvious that the wallet's owner was an American, and most of the Americans in town were there to work on the Olympics.

When I got to the bakery, I managed to explain who I was to the bright, cheery clerk who waited on me. He seemed both happy and relieved as he bowed politely and handed me my wallet, now artfully wrapped and tied with a ribbon. I smiled, bowing slightly and, I hoped, politely, and said "Thank you very much, this is very kind of you," hoping his English was better than my Japanese.

Continuing my walk up the broad boulevard, the mile or so to Zen Koji Temple, I passed the Nagano Post Office, a Kabuki theater, and a couple of department stores and small restaurants. The street scene was an interesting mixture of classical Japanese and modern-day American cultures—Kabuki Theater and a Mr. Donut Shop, looking across the street at each other. On the crowded streets of Nagano on this warm, sunny day, I felt like I was the only Westerner in the city. The international crowds had not yet begun to arrive.

At intersections, the "WALK/DON'T WALK" lights were augmented with music, to let the visually impaired know when they could enter the walkway. I passed a square where workers were building the stage and bleachers for awards ceremonies during the Olympics. The construction activity drew a large crowd of onlookers. As I walked along, distracted by the sights and sounds of the city, I was startled by a young girl, maybe eight or ten years old, as she touched me gingerly and said, in her best grade-school English, "Scuze me sir, scuze me sir," When I stopped and looked at the little girl, I noticed her mother standing about ten feet away, smiling apologetically. The little girl wanted to have her picture taken with me. Her mother explained that the children had been told in school to try to make friends with the foreigners so that they would think highly of Nagano and Japan; the little girl was just doing her homework. I said "Of course, I'd be honored," and posed with the little ambassador. I wanted her to think highly of me as well; maybe now, almost twenty years later, we think of each other every once in a while.

Zen Koji Temple is more than a building; it's a holy campus, a village with its own post office. The fine gravel walkway that begins at the huge iron entry gate passes between rows of shops and stalls. The smell of smoke-fires, coming from the cooking pits and metal forges behind the shops, hangs in the air. Presiding over it all, the ancient temple sits on a hill, overlooking the campus, the city, and the whole valley.

Reaching the temple entrance required a final climb up ten steep steps. It took a fair amount of work to get up to the temple, but a million people a year made the effort, most of them old. So, there I was, standing in front of a 1300-year-old sacred Buddhist temple, built 600 years before the medieval gothic cathedrals of Europe.

I stood there and tried to appreciate the moment, much as I had in Paris kneeling in Notre Dame, or in New York City looking up at the Empire State Building, or in Brazil at Iguaçu Falls. Yes, Zen Koji was impressive. All guidebook destinations were. But I didn't feel anything more profound than the dull satisfaction of putting a check in one more box. I went to the meditation garden on the east side of the temple and sat quietly on one of the stone benches. I reminded myself that I was at an ancient and holy site, and probably wouldn't ever be there again. But honestly, none of it did much for me. I was still just there at a tourist site, like all those other people, looking at something—much like being in a museum.

What really occupied my thoughts and moved my soul while I sat on that bench was the little girl who wanted to have her picture taken with me, and the clerk in the bakery as he handed me that exquisitely wrapped present. And I thought about the Mr. Donut Shop I had passed on the way up to the temple. During the Olympics, the Mr. Donut Shop bags in Nagano were decorated with pastel-colored drawings of little children's faces, always a boy and a girl, smiling sweetly out from the bag. There were endearing little sayings on the bags, things like "love and peace to you please," "we are love one another," "please a happy and joyous day for you ..." all translated into the best English they could manage.

I thought about the old husband and wife farmers, bent over their rakes and hoes, in those fields in the Chikuma Valley. And I thought about last night, at the dragon ceremony in Shinonoi.

Yesterday was Friday, a Japanese religious holiday of some kind, and there was something going on in the village, something big. It wasn't a workday, so I didn't have my Japanese co-workers to explain it, and of course, I couldn't read any of the signs. It was early morning and something was up. There were far more people in little Shinonoi than there usually are on a Friday morning, and everybody was scurrying about. By mid-day, the whole village was festooned with ribbons and banners. Large groups of people began congregating, and they seemed to be gathering in two separate groups, at opposite ends of the village. Each group seemed to be busy constructing something that looked like a long snake, stretched out along the street, for several blocks. The snakes were made of fabric and painted in wild patterns, with the snake at the east end of town being predominantly red and the snake at the western end being mostly green. The process of constructing and laying out the snakes went on all morning and part of the afternoon. As the day wore on, more people arrived on the scene, mostly men, all of them dressed in the age-old battle costumes of the samurai warrior. Midway through the afternoon, one of the important supporting characters in the unfolding drama showed up—Sake! A great deal of the passion that gripped the participants as this drama unfolded was fueled by the sake cup.

Sometime later in the afternoon, the samurai warriors began to get under the "snakes." They lifted the creature over their heads, lowered it down over their bodies, and voila ... they weren't snakes at all—they were dragons! At the front of each dragon sat a gigantic, fearsome dragon head—a fire-breathing, snarling, glaring dragon head. The head was huge and fearsome and a full ten feet off the ground. Just behind the heads of both dragons sat a throne, an ornate, canopied throne, high above the ground—and empty. The dragons, now complete, came alive. The huge, fierce head was attached to a long, writhing body, which had hundreds of white-footed legs showing beneath it—just the lower halves of the legs. I couldn't imagine what it was like under there—they couldn't see anything, and it was hot; it was summer. And finally, samurai warriors surrounded the dragons, complete with headbands painted in the color of their dragon, and samurai swords strapped to their sides. They were real swords, not fakes. And the dance began.

The dragons began moving through the village, winding through the streets, but never quite coming together. One dragon would pass a street corner and pause, trying to decide which way to go. After a moment's deliberation, the dragon might turn right. Minutes later the other dragon would appear, coming from another direction and arriving at the same intersection, look around, and think about which way to turn. He would turn the other way. The dragons were trying to find one another. This went on for hours, with the dragons coming ever closer together, never quite making contact, but moving inexorably to their inevitable confrontation. The crowds lining the streets cheered-on their personal favorite, while the attending samurai warriors fortified themselves with sake. Each dragon contingent seemed to have several samurai warriors whose job it was to keep the sake cups filled, and many in the crowd had brought their own cups; there seemed to be an unlimited supply of sake coming from somewhere.

As the sun began to set, the dragons met in the center of town, and the battle began. The battle was to determine who would rule the valley, and who would occupy the empty throne. The throne was for the queen, and the battle's outcome would determine to which throne she would be elevated. The queen sat in waiting on an elevated platform, adorned in the regal attire of a Medieval Japanese Queen, dispassionately watching the battle—the queen bee watching the drones. As the battle raged, the samurai warriors clashing and slashing—convincingly I might add—while the sake warriors ran about throughout the crowd, filling and refilling cups.

I tried to be as inconspicuous as possible, hopefully invisible. I was the only non-Japanese person in the whole village that day, the only one; if there were any other Gaijins in town, I hadn't seen them. Suddenly one of the sake warriors looked directly at me, and a weird look came across his face. He was an older guy, maybe in his sixties or seventies, old enough to remember, perhaps even to have served in, World War II. Let's see, this was 1997; the war was over in 1945— 52 years ago. If he was 20 years old in 1945 that would make him 72 years old today. And he was a very fit looking 72. At that point, a disconcerting thought took shape in my mind; *maybe he's reliving a moment on Iwo Jima, right now.* And here we were, on a street in Shinonoi, Japan, engaged in a mock battle of the forces of good and evil; and there I stood, a living reminder of his moment of shame, 52 years ago. And somehow, he sensed that I was one of *them*, an American Marine. I might be from a new generation, but an ex-Marine nonetheless. He had a very old score to settle. As he lurched toward me, a very real samurai sword in one hand, and a pitcher of sake in the other, I wondered if this was my day of atonement. Was I going to die, right then, right there, on the streets of Shinonoi, in 1997, for things that happened a half century ago on Iwo Jima? Would I die gracefully, doing honor to his ancestors and mine? Had I read too many cheap novels?

Sorry to disappoint, but that wasn't what happened. The look of incredulity on his face was about seeing a visitor standing there in the street, totally sober, with no sake—hell, without even a *cup*! I was a guest in his village and he was horrified at such inhospitality. He immediately produced a sake cup for me, pushed it into my hands, and filled the cup, insisting that I drink it—immediately! And then he re-filled it, then again, and again, whereupon he bowed ceremoniously and moved on to serve other customers.

The battle ended somehow; I have no idea how these things are determined, but they seem to end, somehow. And when they do, there are a lot of theatrics about the winning and the losing. Finally, the queen is ceremoniously elevated to her new throne and paraded around town, amid the wild cheers and well wishes of the drunken revelers. This went on until the wee hours of the morning. At some point during all of this, I decided it might be prudent for me to go quietly back to my apartment and watch discreetly from the balcony.

And the next day, as I sat on the bench at Zen Koji Temple, I realized that being there in Nagano Prefecture, in the mountains of Japan, was about a lot more than visiting a national landmark. In fact, it was hardly about that at all. I was searching for spiritual meaning in the wrong place. Zen Koji Temple was a building, that's all, just a building, albeit a holy one. But visiting the temple was just putting a check in a box. What being here was *really* about was not that building; it was about the people and the experiences. If there was anything spiritual to be found, it was in the present, not the past. It was about those Mr. Donut bags and the little school girl that would show her classmates the picture she had taken with the strange looking foreigner. It was about that young man in the bakery, bowing and handing me my wallet, perfectly gift-wrapped. And it was about the grizzled old WWII veteran who chose to fill my sake cup, completely forgetting, or at least forgiving, whatever may have happened on one of those islands back in 1945.

Author Biography

Marty Silverthorne

Marty Silverthorne holds degrees from St. Andrews Presbyterian College and East Carolina University.

He has published seven chapbooks including his latest *Holy Ghosts of Whiskey* and forthcoming *Naming the Scars,* the 2017 Longleaf Press Chapbook winner. He has received several grants from the North Carolina Arts Council and in 2015 he won the North Carolina Poetry Society Poet Laureate Award.

Marty's poems have appeared in over 100 journals including *North Carolina Literary Review, Tar River Poetry, St. Andrews Review,* and others.

Reflections Competition
Poetry Juror

Hank at King

for Shelby Stephenson

By Marty Silverthorne

I'm sitting in King's BBQ, stared down on
by an old Republican president, arms wrapped
around Mr. King and a wrinkled-faced black man
in bib overalls. King's barbecue sandwich is alright
but it ain't Paul's or Skylight's.
Somewhere above the farmers, carpenters,
and mechanics eating combo plates
and slurping sweet tea, I hear Hank Sr. slipping
out of dusty speakers, honky tonkin'
'round the restaurant. The percussion
of a black man chopping barbecue could be the
thumping upright bass backing Hank as he
brays back, croons the chorus one more time
before the radio drifts away under the clatter of
rattling dishes and waitresses yodeling orders.

It's good to spend a Friday afternoon eating barbecue
among working folks while Hank signs off and
laborers get a refill of sweet tea to go. I dunk
hushpuppies in hot sauce. I'd rather have stick butter,
but sometimes a man lives short of his wishes.

Order up, I hear above the music of the chopping block.
I'd like to order up another round of Hank,
top off tea and dip hot hushpuppies into melted butter.
Instead I'm thinking of you up in Benson
sitting on the porch of the plankhouse looping long
lines full of barbecue, sooner dogs, sour mash
and sweet Linda patting her foot while you pick that Martin.

Liquor House Salvation

By Marty Silverthorne

Moonshine was free at Mary's Place
below Jamesville. You could buy
a chitlin plate heavy with crispy
paper thin cornbread,
yellow mustard potato salad,
and get a Ball jar of white liquor to boot.
Midnight we would take back roads
to avoid blue lights and angry wives
looking for us in our wandering.
Miss Mary would grin at me
with all three teeth and say,
You Jasper's boy ain't you?
He sat right there, sucked back shine,
and slurped down chitlins
many Saturday nights.
You got his long head boy.
When your granddaddy sobered up,
he was the best shine maker
in Martin County, turning mash
into sweet syrup streaming
out of the worm. Shine like his
could make drunkards of us all.
Revenuers almost caught him once,
sneaking down to his still to get that
Blue Diamond Iron Box addressed to
Henry Jasper Leamon Silverthorne.
He swore off liquor that night but
tended a still in Reg Griffin's hayloft,
running water from the well.
I saw it myself, some say it's a lie,
he read the Bible while Hell's
blue fires heated up the whiskey pot.
You look just like him boy; don't
let liquor eat your soul. Fill up on
chitlins, potato salad, and cornbread.

Author Biography

Jonathan Clayborne

Jonathan is the author of *Ten Dollars and a Zippo*, a poetry collection he published in 2017. Clayborne is writing a Southern Gothic novel, which he hopes to publish in 2018. He sometimes writes under the pseudonym S. Kruger, and is a director, co-founder, and screenwriter for Haunted Pamlico, a Halloween-centered organization that makes short horror films. An award-winning print journalist, he left the newspaper field in 2012. He is an entrepreneur focusing on creative writing and other ventures. His contribution to this anthology is an excerpt from his tentatively titled *Garden Journal*, a soon-to-be-published series of reflections and photographs

Reflections Competition
Student Poetry Juror

Excerpt from "Garden Journal"

By Jonathan Clayborne

A brown-and-white-spotted moth with a long proboscis probed the white-moonlight trumpet of a nicotiana. This herb – flowering tobacco – seems somewhat benign, but it can be toxic if ingested. Paradoxically, nicotiana has been analyzed by scientists for its cancer-treatment qualities. A colorful frog sat, Buddha-like, its head poking out of a gap in bordering stone. A dragonfly made tiny-helicopter sounds, stopping to gain its bearings on a pock-marked, igneous rock. The insect was an ancient being perched atop an equally ancient witness to geologic time.

The Frankenstein-lab-made, blight-ridden tomato vines are dying, but their heirloom rivals are free of disease and bearing happily. In other seasons, the heirlooms die first, unable to resist hereditary fickleness, despite having adapted to the local climate. To me, tomato diseases are as mysterious as the wiles of their host plants, which giveth bumper crops and take them away, with no regard for my dietary needs. The healthy vines include potted Cherokee Purples, a cultivar descended from plants raised by natives, who probably carried the seeds from our region down Andrew Jackson's Trail of Tears. The acidic Cherokee Purples – blush pulp, reddish-purple skin, usually with green shoulders – are often described as having a smoky flavor, and there are few joys to compare with the tang of these fruits combined with olive oil, fresh basil and feta cheese on toasted bread, my favorite version of bruschetta.

Two rambunctious boxer-bulldogs insisted on wrestling with me as the dragonfly rose and hovered. The dogs wriggled with infectious joy, licked my face until laughter made me lightheaded. Later, I plucked my first cucumber of the season while hundreds – thousands? – of fireflies made an early Christmas display of the near-summer woods. Cricket sounds joined other night murmurs in quiet chorus. Don't send me away yet. I'm not finished with nature, and she's too willing to hold me in her arms, to sing me into the night.

Author Biography

Beverly Horvath

Playwright Beverly Horvath found a passion for films and stageplays while living in Los Angeles and has participated in many small theatre productions. Beverly now resides in Aurora, NC, and has been writing for screen and stage since 2001. She has written original screenplays, book adaptations for screen and two musical stage-plays while collaborating with talented musicians/lyricists. Her musical play *Whiskey Flats* has been produced in New Bern, North Carolina.

Caged Metal Feathers Synopsis

By Bev Horvath

"Caged Metal Feather" is a full-length movie script by Beverly Horvath. Adapted from the memoirs of Istvan Horvath, it is based on the true story of a boy coming of age amid turmoil in 20th century Hungary. The following is a synopsis of the script.

From a very early age, Istvan Horvath's family described him as an independent cuss; his wandering spirit got him into one adventure after another. From a firsthand account of World War II—as seen through the eyes of a six-year-old—to standing up for his beliefs in the 1956 Hungarian Uprising, he has proven his family was right all along...

1939: At the light of dawn we find toddler Istvan on the family porch, watching a bee gather pollen from a large morning glory blossom. He pets it. The bee slips past Istvan's fat little finger and flies to safety. Istvan is ready to explore his world and climbs down the front steps, stretches high to lift the gate latch and heads down the dirt road. To the surprise of his Godmother, Istvan arrives on her front porch grinning, wearing not a single stitch of clothing.

1944: Townspeople line the main highway into Buda. Istvan and his two brothers wriggle through the crowd and are astonished to see the German military streaming toward town. The boys run home to tell their father about the commotion. Germany is invading Hungary. The war soon encroaches Istvan's world as planes battle above his neighborhood. He is enthralled with the dogfights, deadly maneuvers filling the sky.

1954: Now a handsome young man of sixteen, Istvan attends a rally of promises by the local Communist party. He soon voices his disagreement with the presentation and leaves the rally in disgust. After finding a note in his school papers inviting him to stand up for his beliefs, Istvan joins the Hungarian Indians, a clandestine organization opposing the Soviet occupation. Messages with instructions are then left for him inside a loose brick outside his school. Istvan checks it daily and performs acts against the regime that he could be shot for doing. Even his best friend cannot be told of his activities.

In his quest for freedom, Istvan develops a love for flying and is accepted as a student at Three Borders Mountain Gliderport. He soon becomes entranced by the beautiful Veronika, fiancé of his role model, Geza, and remains involved at the gliderport by learning to operate the launching winch. Istvan is at the winch controls the day tragedy strikes. As Geza's plane is winched aloft it suddenly dives and crashes, killing Geza instantly.

Days after the tragedy, Istvan sits alone at the fire pit when a distraught Veronika approaches. Istvan attempts to comfort her and soon confesses his love. She tries to dissuade him, but then kisses him and leads him off the path to an open glen. It is there she introduces Istvan to the warmth of a woman; it is the last time he will ever see her.

1956: On the fateful morning of October 23, Istvan completes his graveyard shift at the metal works factory. Upon checking his brick "mailbox," he finds an invitation to a rally at the Budapest radio station. Thousands of people are crowding the streets as he nears the site; Hungarians are tired of living under Russian rule and the ill-fated uprising begins. Istvan watches as citizens break into and take over the radio station amid gunfire and shouting. The jubilation is short-lived as Russian troops and tanks invade the city. Istvan and his friends stay and fight throughout the night, becoming separated the next day. After getting shot in the leg, Istvan remains in the city for another night. The following morning he exits the city.

After arriving home, Istvan's mother remains calm even though he is bleeding. Against the wishes of her heart, she advises that he leave Hungary with his older brother, Laci. Much to Istvan's surprise, his best friend Feri accepts his offer to join the journey. The boys head out on foot. After several instances of escaping capture by the Russians, they arrive safely at a refugee camp, in Austria.

But now, a decision is to be made. They agree that they should stay together, but where? One wants to stay in Austria, another prefers France, and the third chooses the United States. It's time to let fate make the decision. Each of the young men tosses a coin into the air. The holder of the odd coin will make the decision... the coins glint as they flip through the air...

The Hatbox Synopsis

By Bev Horvath

"The Hatbox" is an original full-length movie script by Beverly Horvath and has been adapted for the stage. It is a dramatic comedy that tells the extraordinary life of Claire Sinclair-Sutton. The following is the synopsis of the story.

Ninety-year-old Claire Sinclair has mere hours left of her life. She breathes with a whisper as her family gathers at her hospital bed. There is something Claire must tell them, but all she can do is ask for her old tattered hat. Great Grandson Ed proudly delivers a hatbox and hands it over to the room full of characters gathered at Claire's bedside. When the box is opened, instead of a hat, they find memorabilia documenting Claire's colorful past. One by one, the family forages through the age-worn items, but something is missing.

While the family tries to piece Claire's life together, it is Claire herself that tells us her storied past when her memory is prompted by the hatbox contents and the activities of the surrounding family. As we watch her life of struggles and triumphs unfold, the family discovers the amazing life that Claire had experienced.

Young Claire was raised by her widowed immigrant mother during the early 20th century in New York City. While on her annual summer visits to her paternal grandparent's farm, Claire visits the neighbor boy, Edwin Sinclair. They spend many long summer days together.

Tragedy strikes in March 1911 when Young Claire watches from the street below as dozens of women, including her mother, jump to their deaths when trapped on the top floors of a burning clothing factory. Young Claire is taken in by her grandparents and withdraws from the world. It is several months before Young Edwin coaxes her back to reality by challenging her to a race to the schoolhouse. Determined Young Claire cannot turn down a challenge. She bolts past him and runs down the road. He grins and trots after her.

The bond between Claire and Edwin remains throughout their lives, carrying them through the challenges of wartime separation and the fight for a woman's right to vote. It is only during her last day that the family completes the puzzle of clues contained in the old hatbox to discover that Claire truly was an incredible woman, and the surprising family secret she kept until the end.

2017 Annual Competition

The Pamlico Writers Competition was a spring annual juried writing contest featuring adult and student authors. Started in 2013, the final 2017 event featured adult contests in Fiction, Nonfiction, Poetry, and student contests in Prose and Poetry.

First, Second, and Honorary Mention prizes were awarded in the Adult competition while a cash student scholarship was awarded in each student contest.

2017 PWG Competition Winners

Pictured (l to r) Eileen Lettick, Richard Knowles, Linda Bledsoe, Travis Green, and Pamela Desloges. Other winners, Denis Sinar, Deborah Doolittle, Michael Worthington, Sarah Swan, Jo Ann Hoffman, and Student Winners Emani Dunning, and Natalie Valentine were not present.

Author Biography

Dennis Sinar

Dennis has been a listener nearly all his life. Working as a physician, listening was essential to making an accurate diagnosis and so stories about people provided ample material.

He has published two short story collections titled *Not Born Here* about the fictional characters that live in Marsden, North Carolina. These are stories told by people you would meet on the street in any Southern town and describe their highs and lows with life, love, and family. Roger and Patrice, a retired couple from Boston, link the stories as they struggle to understand the ways of the South.

2017 Competition
Fiction First Place

The Doctor in Town

By Dennis Sinar

Fate, the mother of us all, guided me here in 1957. I drove a dusty 1950 power glide Chevy into town looking for a job. Cars parked at angles studded the four blocks of Main Street and shoppers crowded both sides of the street. Eventually, I found a vacant two-story building at the north end of town, a block beyond the established stores. Negotiations were quick. The owner needed a tenant, and the combination first-floor office and second-floor apartment were suitable for a businessman who didn't mind being on the edge of town. Location was not a problem for my business because people would come. It took a day to find a sign-maker and hang my shingle above the door. Carl Jordan, M.D. was open for business. I was the only doctor in town.

In the late 1950s, a general practitioner in a small town was expected to be a caring, gentle, knowledgeable person who listened to his patients, and most importantly, he was a person willing to work hard. People came with the usual illnesses and in that first year, my practice grew as I established trust. My patients received competent care during office hours and in most emergencies. I took care of any patient, black or white, rich or poor, ornery or not. And I made house calls. If a drunk wandered onto my porch on a Saturday night, he sat there until he was sober. Then I saw him first when the office opened. My posted office hours were eight to five, five days a week, but that was only a guideline. If a sick patient knocked after hours, I yelled out the upstairs window for them to sit on the porch and I'd be down shortly.

Most patients were my neighbors and it was easy to remember all of the family illnesses. I treated mostly common diseases in those families and sat with other families for comfort when their people died. I learned that the interview with the patient was the most important part of the encounter. People needed to tell their story on their own terms and it was best to smile, nod and listen as they talked.

I learned that it was important to observe all the clues in the encounter. I remember a wife who was nervously waiting for my diagnosis of her husband's illness. As she sat, she rubbed her trembling index finger across the hair of her eyebrow and then repeated the motion on the other eyebrow. She sat silently beside her husband, looking between us. To hide his embarrassment, he looked straight ahead at the sunset print on the wall, studying the print and the colors of the sunset. He was used to facing the sun in tobacco fields, and his face was lined with crows feet. His right foot tapped, tapped on the floor to some rhythm in his head. The wife looked at her husband and then back to me, willing him to talk about his symptoms, to be truthful about his weight loss, lack of appetite, and the pains in his stomach. He was most often silent, not ready, so she told the story. I watched her hands and her eyes for clues as to what she needed. It was obvious that he had a cancer of some kind, likely terminal. He never looked at me.

Before I said the words, she knew her suspicions were true, and her eyes asked what could be done. She wanted my guidance on the path from here to there, but he never looked at me. Diagnosing cancer was terrible, but not difficult. Someone with a wasting disease, steady pain, and jaundice had the bad disease. Finding where the cancer was located was not important back then. People did not want to know the kind of cancer; they just accepted that it was cancer, an untreatable condition in their mind. Every day they stayed above ground was a blessing, a day to be used to work and provide for their family for as long as they were able.

In those early days, my hands were my greatest asset, warm, smooth, and neatly groomed. Someone told me that people didn't trust a doctor with dirty hands and so I washed my hands after coming into the room so the patients knew they were clean. In the beginning, it was difficult for me to examine patients because I disliked physical contact, but when people complimented my gentle touch, I became more comfortable.

Examining a patient was like playing a fine instrument, my warm hands started well away from the tender area and slowly worked toward their particular area of tenderness. During the exam, I nodded often to encourage patients to add details to their story. If someone complained of pain in their chest, I'd gently palpate the back and front, feeling for tender spots. If I found tenderness, it was the end of my search and I knew what to do; if not, I'd listen with my scope and decide on something different. If their chest rattled, they went home with pills dispensed by the nurse from our back office supply; if their chest was quiet, they went home with the same pills, but a different color. The results were the same—patients most often got better. My capsules looked different, large or medium sized and colored blue, white, or bright yellow. It was easy to buy colored double o wax capsules out of town and fill them with sugar. Placebo pills were common at the time, and as the nurse handed the patient their envelope of pills, she instructed them to swallow them whole, so they never tasted the sugar. I used simple medicines because they worked.

The mechanics of laboratory testing did not interest me, I was concerned only with the mystery and the manifestations of disease. My medical knowledge was refined by trial and error. On a back office shelf was my single reference, the Merck Manual. I consulted it with difficult cases and the pages became worn over the years. In most cases, the manual proved adequate.

Most days I was able to puzzle out a patient's problem using common sense. My treatments reinforced the placebo principle— examine carefully, treat with confidence, and expect a cure.

Surprisingly, their confidence in me was the most effective medicine. If a patient believed I knew how to treat their problem, their belief was enough; patients tried to get better because it was expected. When people heard my diagnosis, they nodded understanding, and symptoms that were unbearable before the visit, with my reassurance, became bearable. I had a nervous tic, rubbing my knuckles back and forth across my lips and teeth as I thought about a difficult case. The tic initially gave patients a start, but then eventually instilled confidence in my diagnostic skills. The tic helped solve a surprising number of vexing problems.

Vaccination of children was not widespread in the South. I learned that childhood diseases, whether in a rich child or a poor child mostly improved in a day or two, and if not, I sent the patient on to a specialist in Wilmington. In children what looked like a cold might actually be a serious disease like polio or meningitis and could get much worse in more than a few days. Those were the times of the most severe cases of polio, widespread tuberculosis, and the worst of a handful of other severe childhood illnesses. Thankfully, those times have passed. When I sent patients to the city, the specialists appreciated the prompt referral and always let me know how things turned out.

Payment for my services was a challenge because few people had readily available cash. Most offered trades or asked for credit until their crops came in. I collected food, dressed farm animals, or canned preserves. Patients saved their best harvest for the doctor. If I took care of all three kids in a family for their colds, I might get a smoked ham; if a farmer's wife had the vapors, the husband brought a few thick steaks. When I had enough food, I took handmade clothing.

In the practice of general medicine, people came to the office with common ailments: colds, scrapes, arthritis, and fevers. Emergencies and house calls always came in the middle of the night for patients too sick to leave their bed. An emergency for a farmer had the same importance whether it was a cow in labor or his wife's spells. Often I would see the wife and the cow on the same house call. In both cases, I prescribed the same pills, and more often than not, the wife and the cow got better. I saw joy, grief, and the loss of life, often in the same week.

Toward the end of a long day, I was exhausted and failed in my caring. The best I could do at those times was to follow the thread of their history, but no diagnosis came into my head. I saw the person in front of me as a skeleton stripped of skin or a blob of muscles that talked. When that happened, I asked them to come back in the morning for a fresh look. People saw my foibles and believed my words both in town and in the office.

One morning, a car weaving down Main Street hit a man, and the patrons of the Starlight grill had an excellent view of the accident. I was sitting at a table in the front window, looked out at the splattered man, and then resumed my breakfast, knowing the man was already dead and beyond my services. None of the patrons questioned my decision.

Through weeks, then years, I learned to appreciate the strength of the human body—the oldest to the youngest bodies—and how they adapted as they aged. It was common to see an old granny and then a newborn baby, one after the other in a morning, and the diversity of life amazed me.

There were many times when I went to a person's home, often in the middle of the night. On one visit, the spouse opened the front door, nodded, and led me upstairs to their bedroom. It was a clean room but infused with the smell of sickness. On the wall opposite the window, there was a huge poster bed with a white lace canopy. The patient, a man I had seen only rarely, was propped up in the bed, leaning against large feather pillows, his breathing so labored that he could barely get more than a few words out without pausing. There was an odor of urine from the bed and damp washed sheets hung out the window to dry. By way of decoration in the room, hanging on a nail in the middle of the wall across from the bed was a crayon drawing of a man. Underneath the drawing in a child's handwriting was: To Dear Papa. This man was Papa.

One hot summer afternoon, a woman sat in the office and told me about her husband: "That man is disturbed, sick you know. He's never been all there, what with staring into space rather than looking me in the eye like a normal person, talking crazy sentences about the devil or someone following him or trying to poison him. He never tells normal things anymore, and people stay well away from him. I've never known for him to hurt anybody, but with crazy people, you never know when they're just going to snap and go for your throat."

She went on in that vein for some time, and I found that letting her get it out was the best tonic, nodding, looking at her face and listening with my hands crossed in my lap. Eventually, her tape ran out and she went back into herself. Our conversation continued, but she avoided my eyes and looked down at my hands as if they would give the diagnosis and what she should do.

Then, one week, my routine changed. Odd feelings stirred in me, and I felt something alive moving deep inside my abdomen, tightening and squeezing, not yet pain but becoming pain. The feeling became worse and changed to pain in another week. I had examined enough patients to know the diagnosis, but not how long. My nurse and I decided to close the office gradually over the next two months. I knew there was no treatment, even in the big city. At home, I turned to thoughts of God and an afterlife.

I became philosophical about the extremes of life, knowing that the boundary between life and death could be measured like the narrow path of a tornado, and like the tornado, my disease was unstoppable. My ego hoped that perhaps medicine might hold back that boundary and that my will alone could determine the path enough for it to miss me. With each day and as the pain increased, the division between life and death became narrower, making me wonder about the next adventure. A week after the office closed, I sat in the sun on the front porch and looked at my hands. I was surprised at how bony they had become, how the flesh had stripped away. The knuckles were prominent, and the skin was stretched tight around every joint, yet I believed that my grip was still strong and my gentle touch was the same touch that so many patients recalled. Maybe it was true.

I had seen life end in suddenness, a merciful transition between living and then not, and I had seen the opposite—a slow, painful process of ending that fostered replaying, regret, and only a few pleasant memories. Which path would I prefer if it were in my power? My preference didn't matter because the choice was made for me.

Perhaps my legacy will live on, but I doubt it. After I'm gone, people will forget the good and only remember the bad of their dealings with me. My greatest secret would go with me to the grave. On my scout drive into town in 1957, I was looking for easy money but instead found my destiny on a path that was irreversible. In the end, if people thought I was a doctor and helped

Author Biography

Travis Green

Travis Green is an aspiring novelist in the fields of horror and speculative fiction. Following in the footsteps of literary pioneers such as Ira Levin, Ray Bradbury, and Richard Matheson, his stories are most often at home in the twilight between the real world and that of the fantastic. He lives in New Bern, North Carolina, where he is currently at work on a new novel.

2017 Competition
Fiction Second Place

The Anomaly

By Travis Green

Perseverance.

It's something I see long forgotten in the faces of our town. It's in the eyes, mostly. It's when I pass them on the street and they glare at me beneath wisps of snow-blown hair, and I know they've forgotten what it means to survive. For those of us who've been around long enough, however, we know better.

Yes, we know.

We were all taught a little something about that—about sucking it up, and pushing on through—back when we were green and star-eyed, and still had plenty of our best years ahead. And as I linger here at the window of time looking back on that magical summer, I can still make out the rime etching spider webs up the glass, can see those first breaths of morning fogging the air like some ghostly vision of halitosis, just as they had all those years ago...

Things were different back then. Sure, it's a platitude—but it also happens to be true. Hunterfield was a simpler town in those days, belonged to a simpler world. Our family woke well before sunrise to milk Bessie and feed the hungry horses; yet we were merely cogs of a much greater communal organism, a bright country where front porches stayed crowded and screen doors left unlocked, where children kicked rusty cans and ran wild in the streets. The usual cash crops—tobacco, soybeans, corn—lay sprawled through the center of town, the harbors lining the coast and dotted by legendary fleets of Hunterfield trawlers, names scrawled down their sides in flaky hard-boiled script: THE BOUNTY. SCAVENGER. EDWARD TEACH ENTERPRISE.

Festivals highlighted the year, the Tulips & Lager Parade in March, followed as always by the Blessing of the Fleet and, mother of all galas, the Croaker Festival—a time when families strolled the boardwalk and watched the Fourth of July fireworks before crowding to see which young miss nabbed the title of Croaker Queen. The men downed another Coors as their gals whistled for street dances and the band cranked "Brown-Eyed Girl" out into the night; children tossed firecrackers and ran barefoot over the Oriental bridge, water lapping beneath them as they pointed to the wild neon of jellyfish and man-of-wars and of their own imagination.

Then were the forever-lasting brownouts which haunted the town year-round. Occasionally it was the East Enders—Florence and Whortonsville and Paradise Shoals—occasionally the Aurora side, though most times the entire town was thrown into the blackness, hurled headfirst. Families collected ceremoniously under grandparents' roofs to swap yawns and play charades, or perhaps gather in hushed candlelit vigils to whisper old ghost stories. And later that night, as the crickets gabbed and the frogs told tall tales, everyone tossed and turned in the swelter of these dilapidated screen-door palaces.

Those nights if you yellowed your sheets it came out so warm it burned...

Even Hunterfield-then was not immune to tragedy, however, and folks carried with them their weight of draughts and bad days. Yet even our darkest moments were only the usual sordid legends of adultery, occasional suicides, mishap deaths. But there was also the chance old-time murder, most of these rarely as simple as a flared temper or barroom brawl but usually the culmination of a slow, steady slide into depression and, ultimately, madness.

Yes, that was the way things were.

Before.

As I sit here peeling away the layers of that summer, like the layers of some bitter onion, I recall that the first warnings were from the fishermen. Even these were slow in coming—but so, I suppose, was the storm itself. And yet in a way, I believe we all felt it coming, felt it *growing*, if not in the air then perhaps in our own skittish hearts. One morning you turned from the closet and, rather than the ripped-knee coveralls and white-tee you'd decided on, instead found yourself clutching a winter jacket...mittens...a toboggan.

First was Mark Halpern down on Acorn Avenue, talking in his

sleep, blathering away with tears in his eyes about freezing nights on the water—nights so cold he's sure it was *ice* he'd heard scratching at the hull. Then it was old Tommy Rafferty, who'd left a leg in Korea and was first to call attention to the strange flock migrations in the area, pointing ominously as speckles of Mallards and swan winged away from the docks.

The stories escalated when the crew of the ALBEMARLE ELITE reported a hailstorm of frightening violence in the Sound; pictures of injuries received were documented in the local *Clarion*. From then it seemed we could all sense the nights becoming cooler, the days after that, and finally, it was as if Hunterfield fell into a deep blue dream. Pipes burst. The sun lost its strength. Crops began to frost and worried farmers prepared to cut their losses and plow.

They wouldn't have the chance.

The night of August 28th—two weeks after the hailstorm first appeared in the weeklies, and after light hours of back and forth sleet—the town of Hunterfield witnessed its first flake of genuine summer snowfall. Many more followed, and by morning the slush had topped four inches. School was canceled, at which time wild half-dressed children blazed from their homes, mouths blurting high nonsensical cries that tore through the streets like gunfire.

The rest of us only looked on in grave awe and wonder...some even fear.

The snowfall continued through the day and into night, pausing once to catch its breath and then never looking back. By next morning, the toll stood at eighteen inches. Still, the blizzard raged, sweeping in from the darkness that settled over the Sound and piling snow in great heaps on doorsteps and beneath windows, flanking cars, burying roads. The looming sign as you entered town, WELCOME TO HUNTERFIELD WE SLEEP WITH THE FISHES!, was now covered in white and said nothing.

Reporters and press deluged the town; tabloids were printed, offering the truth of *"The Arctic Bubble of North Carolina"* or its purported effects, *"Hunterfield Residents Growing Fur!!!"*. The mystery of Hunterfield had become a national obsession, and soon we all began groping unnaturally for ways to handle this newfound fame.

Some came forward with tall tales of life *out there*. Oh yes, they'd seen them, the lights in the sky, and THEY were the ones responsible. Some said it was nothing short of a rebuke from the Almighty; others claimed it an "unprecedented weather anomaly" and left it at that. There was talk of the next Ice Age and one family—the Redmans—really did leave town and never returned. They're getting along well now in Atlanta.

And yet, like so many pop culture fads before it, interest waned and the Arctic Hull of Hunterfield quietly faded away, vanishing into the dark night of America's subconscious. For residents of Hunterfield, however, life did not change as the fad did. Summer wore on and ended. Winter came and went, with no lull in activity but thankfully no increase. Interest waned, but the snow did not; it remained and still remains to this day.

Longer piers were installed down at the harbors with federal grant money, a reckoning of the massive ice floes that have collected along the shore. Defying the weather, our fishermen trudged forth with admirable determination, continuing to serve the waters and thereby feed hungry mouths waiting back at home.

It was the farmers, however, who took the brunt of the hit—and what a hit it was.

The bulk of that growing season was lost, buried under ice, and for the next few years, it appeared the fields would never be resurrected. My own father had passed away by then, my brother and I going our separate ways in the farm supply and construction businesses, respectively. The anomaly crippled him initially, but lately business has been picking up. Others have made allowances, as well; only eight months ago, the miser Earl Hutchins completed what is said to be something of a greenhouse—big as two football stadiums, complete with the latest-day sprinkler systems and heat lamps and doors wide enough to let in the Cub tractors and combines. It's going well. Others quickly followed suit.

Of the one hundred counties in this state, only seven are currently being affected by the anomaly, with three of those in it up to their elbows—none as bad as ours. There's been talk of taking down the hothouses and stopping all attempts at growing; at this writing, the idea is in the minority, though the conversation itself shows just how much things have changed since the anomaly first hit. Tourism has suffered and is close to being pronounced dead. That was a concern in the early years when the first of the Roswell-like groups dwindled to pairs. But we've moved on. Sad to say, there's much more to see in this Tar Heel State than our small white corner of the universe.

I am sitting at the window now as I write this, and looking out can see the barn where I shared my first kiss, the fence where I broke my first bone: the bitter and the sweet. My hair is white now and not the rusty brown it was for oh, some fifty years or more, but that's not the snow.

Just age, that's all.

Nights like these I wake sometimes, crawl out of bed. My wife is asleep beside me but she doesn't stir, not anymore. She's used to it by now—used to *me*, I should say, and my tendency to roam after dark. And some nights as I sit here looking out I still dream about the old days, about skipping stones and closed clams on the lake, and of crowded clotheslines on a balmy mid-afternoon. I dream about the dance of vapors over burning asphalt or the sweet miserable feeling of the dog days of summer. I dream so many things. But even I know that's all these are, and all they'll ever be...

Dreams.

END

Author Biography

Pam Desloges

Pam grew up in the mountains of New Hampshire and spent much time on the rugged coast of Maine. After retiring from a small New England college, she lost interest in shoveling snow. She now lives in New Bern, North Carolina, with her husband, Max. She has been published in the anthology *Art Inspires Poetry*, the blog *Polly's Tea Kettle*, and a magazine for dog lovers, *Sniff & Barkens*. She is a member of the North Carolina Writers Network, the Pamlico Writer's Group, and is a founding member of the Neuse River Writers' Group.

Find her work at: https://www.facebook.com/pamdesloges

2017 Competition
Fiction Honorable Mention

David Walsh Is Dead

By Pamela Desloges

When Ellie couldn't sleep one night, she got out of bed at 2:00 am and went downstairs. Her thoughts skimmed across thin ice, and she wondered where they would fall in: getting the Nissan inspected, seeing the grandkids on Saturday, the black spot on her toenail, the winter pansies recuperating from the surprise frost. Her mind stopped and did a pirouette on her high school days: brick building on the hill, cinderblock hallways, girls hugging textbooks to their chests, the house on Cross Street, the flower garden in their backyard. David.

In 1965, just before she started high school, her family had moved to Waldeboro, a small town on the coast of Maine. Her brother, Chris, a year older than she, was one grade ahead. He was her opposite. She was shy, always unsure, an A+ student, an obedient child. He lived headlong, fixed and drove cars, stayed out late at night, drank beer, and charmed the room. She wanted to be like him but might as well have wanted to fly.

She made a few friends in this new high school—Carol and Barbara, who were shy, like her. They had quiet adventures and fragile fantasies. They read *Hamlet* together and acted it out. Life was small for them.

Ellie knew no other way to live, except in reading. She devoured books. They were her real life: Dickens, Walter Farley, Albert Payson Terhune, Tennyson, O'Henry. Books about dogs and horses, kings and orphans, love and triumph.

Sometime that first year, Chris and David became friends. They spent many evenings and weekends at her house, laughing in the kitchen, telling stories to her Dad. Sometimes, they came into the living room and sang along as she foot-pumped the old player piano. The boys' arms around each other, they could have been a Rockwell painting. She basked in their aura.

Ellie did not date, but she had many male friends. She was "one of the guys." She was their confidante, their sister, their chum. Their girlfriends were not jealous of her because she was not attractive or flirty. She was solid, plain, and safe. A classmate, Sandra, once said to her, "If I ever die, I'd like Tom to go out with you." *Because then he would never forget Sandra.*

Ellie and David became close friends. If no one else was home when David showed up, he would stay anyway and talk with her. They shared certain dreams: a small farm with a few animals and a vegetable garden, writing a book, traveling the world, seeing the Beatles live. He would stay for hours, talking while she washed the dishes, sometimes helping her, moving furniture while she vacuumed or helping her fold clothes. He said more than once, "Don't you ever tell anyone I did this." They often sat on the curb in front of the house, talking about books they had recently read or movies that the other HAD to see. She fell in love with him.

David dated. He had a "reputation." One of the older girls in his large circle of friends took Ellie aside in front of Woolworths one day. "Be careful," she said. "He only wants one thing from girls." Ellie knew what she meant, but could not conceive of David wanting that from her. In fact, Ellie (feeling that she would tragically die at the age of 18) had two wishes in her life: that she would go to Wales before she died and that David would kiss her. She firmly believed that Wales was more likely.

Her first date was with Michael, for her Junior Prom. She didn't have another date until her senior year, and that was with Matt—bowling.

David floated in and out of her life. He graduated and got a job at the local hardware store. She kept busy with school, babysitting, and cleaning houses for money.

The summer after her high school graduation, Ellie got a job at the Lotta Rock Dairy Bar. She worked afternoons and evenings. Her overnights and mornings were spent as a companion for a 96-year-old woman who had a huge house on Bartlett Hill. The woman's niece paid Ellie $50 a week to live with Mona and keep an eye on things. Mona was able to maintain herself, but the niece worried that she might fall, and wanted to know that someone would be there to pick her up and call an ambulance. Ellie watched in fascination every night as Mona stood at her picture window facing the ocean, pointed the tip of her cane at the sky and jabbed at it.

"Shoot! Shoot the moon!" Then she clumped up the stairs, Ellie following behind.

David took her out a few times, but they were more like pals than sweethearts. They would ride around and talk. Then stop at the dam and talk, or go to Forest Lake and talk. She enjoyed every minute with him.

One night, he picked her up from work to drive her home. They talked in the car outside the house. She started to get out, and he said, "Can I ask you a question?" She said, "What?" He said, "Can I kiss you?"

She slid back into the car, and let herself fully experience the dream of her life. It was not a passionate kiss, but a sweet one: innocent and lingering. She became dizzy. He said, "Good night, now." She said nothing and melted out to the sidewalk. He waited until she went in the side door, then drove off.

She didn't hear from him for a few weeks. Then he called to say he was drafted into the Army. She didn't see him before he left. That summer, she went out with a variety of boys and men: Cliff, the head chef at the restaurant where she waitressed; Rodney, who had been in theater class with her; Peter, who had just gotten out of juvenile detention; Michael, her date from the Junior Prom.

David went to Vietnam, along with so many of her male friends. Through her brother, she got his mailing address and wrote to him. He was delighted to get her letter, and they wrote back and forth for a year. Her letters were funny and light—the kind a sister or cousin would write. His letters were filled with his observations and feelings about his experiences there. He asked if he could take her out when he got home.

While David was overseas, her family moved to a town about two hours south. She was a sophomore at the university when he returned from Vietnam. She hoped he would come to visit on campus, but he never did. When she was home for Christmas vacation, he called and came to her house, and they went out on an actual date, dinner at a local restaurant.

She was nervous, wishing that it was not a date. Wanting it to be like the old days, when they were comfortable together. They didn't talk much, each waiting for the other to say something. She ached inside, feeling like he was still far away in Vietnam. That was the last time she saw him.

Later that year, she heard that he had married. A friend of a friend of his told her. Inwardly she raged. *He should have told me; he's a coward!* More than that, he should have loved her. She knew nothing about the girl he married and did not want to know. She flung herself into activities and relationships and became the person she had always wanted to be. She went to political rallies and parties, wore leather fringe, engaged in discussions with professors during class, and drank vodka. She enjoyed this new life as she let the world open to her. It felt wonderful to dare to do new things. She lost her shyness and discovered that people liked her.

After college graduation, Ellie married (as all her friends did), worked at a few careers, had a child and got divorced. Her life became full, rewarding, always interesting.

Every now and then over the years (maybe on a snowy winter walk), she would think of David and what he might be doing. *Do they have children? Are they still married? Where does he live now? What is his job? Did he ever stop smoking?* She had no way of finding these things out because all of their mutual friends were now far removed from her. Her brother had not kept in touch with David. Then she would get distracted by her dog digging at something in the snow, and forget about these ponderings.

Sometimes she thought about driving up to Waldeboro for a day and poking around. Look in the phonebook, go to the library, search town records. See if she could bump into any people who knew him. The trip was a fantasy, shored up by a scenario of long-lost love reuniting. The fantasy was more alluring than reality, so she kept putting off the trip.

She always hoped that he was doing well, that he loved his kids and they loved him. That he liked his job and made a good living. That he was happy. Most of all, that he was happy. She never stopped loving him and, despite her initial anger, never wished him ill.

She raised her daughter, got her master's degree, worked at a small college for 20 years, and retired. Then she moved to North Carolina and met Steven.

That night when she couldn't sleep, she got up and sat on the couch with her laptop. She started searching, using all the free locators and search engines. After a few hours, she had found very little: only David's name. Three towns where he had lived (all very close to their high school). The date of his death: March 11, 2000. Sixteen years ago, when he would have been 58.

She felt the loss of decades. *Dead all these* years. *How could I not have known?* Now a void, where possibility had stood.

The next morning, as she sat at her desk in the upstairs office, she saw Steven crossing the 17th fairway, clubs jangling, on his way home. Six years married to this kind, wonderful man. She felt a peace, like an old oak drawer sliding smoothly into place. Resting where it belongs, quietly and securely. She went downstairs and poured him a cup of decaf. The clink of his golf clubs made a music that was like a theme song.

Later in the afternoon, they sat at her laptop, planning their trip for the summer. He had already chosen the courses he wanted to play in Scotland. Now they were working on the second part of the trip. He peered at the Internet map. "How long does it take to get to Wales, I wonder?"

She stroked his finger.

Long time.

Author Biography

Eileen Lettick

Eileen is a former elementary classroom teacher and staff developer. After 30 years in the classroom, she continued her mission in literacy—changing readers into writers. Eileen has presented literacy workshops to teachers and administrators on the east coast from New Hampshire to Florida. She maintains her literacy resource website for parents, teachers, and students-- scribbles-n-lit.org. Her own writing, whether fiction, nonfiction, or poetry, often develops through the eyes of strong female characters.

Eileen won the 2017 award for nonfiction at the Pamlico Writers' Conference for her memoir, *The Poetry Lesson*. Her middle-grade time travel novel, *Sarah the Bold*, as yet unpublished, placed as a finalist for the 2012 Tassy Walden New Voices in Children's Literature Book Award. Eileen has published poems in *The Teacher's Anthology* of Creative Communications and in the July 2017 issue of *Wallingford Magazine*. Her article, *May the Road Rise up to Meet You* appeared in the 2013 July *Challenge Magazine*. She is presently completing a young adult novel, *My Life on Roller Skates*.

A Connecticut transplant, Eileen lives in Chocowinity, North Carolina and is an active member of the Pamlico Writers' Group. She enjoys sailing down the Pamlico River with her husband, choral singing, and of course, writing and reading.

The Poetry Lesson

By Eileen Lettick

The lesson took place one warm October morning when the scent of trees changing colors wafted through the tall open windows of my fifth-grade classroom at Saint John School. I sat dead center in front of Sister Mary Leonto who was hunkered down at her desk, her ear cocked against a battered tan radio listening to Paul Harvey's morning news program. She let out a low snort of laughter as Paul closed the show with his signature "Good day?" The program had become as much a part of our morning exercises as the Hail Mary and Pledge of Allegiance. "Children, Mr. Harvey is both humorous and informative," Sister would say.

As with every morning preceded by a teacher workshop day, Sister Leonto, looked refreshed, informed, and ready to change the world. In her precise voice, she announced to all 36 of us, "Boys and girls, today...we will learn poetry."

Poetry! I thought. I had always wanted to learn poetry. I wiggled a little in my seat, sat up straight, and folded my hands on my desk to let Sister know I was ready for action. I waited anxiously and wondered just how she would transform us into poets in one easy lesson. My eyes followed her black and white silhouette as she strode to the chalkboard.

S-p-r-i-n-g the good sister wrote clearly across the blackboard. She turned to the class and delivered a forceful "Spring!" that sent droplets of spit dancing across John Boland's desk. "Who can give me a word that rhymes with spring?"

All 36 of us clamored to be first. Our hands raised politely, but our hearts jockeyed for position, our eyes silently pleading. *Call on me, Sister! Call on me!* She wove her way through the rows of desks, and one after another, we responded in turn. "Swing...bring...sing...sting."

"Wonderful, boys and girls! Wonderful!" She gave a triumphant smile. She tossed out another word, "Lip."

"Pip...chip...tip...rip...nip." We were a class on fire, crazed and reveling in our rhymes. We were Longfellows dedicated solely to pleasing our dear Sister Leonto.

The nun skipped across the classroom floor. "Oh you dear children, I knew you would be good at this! Now keep in mind that poetry is simply thoughts put to rhyme. A poem tells a story, so what we need to do today is to make up a little rhyming story. And since it's so close to Halloween," she rubbed her palms together and lowered her voice, "let's make up a scary poem."

"Oooh," we all said in unison. A nun being scary. This is pretty cool, I thought. I wondered what other ideas she had up those long black sleeves.

"Children, I'll start you off with the first line." In her impeccable penmanship, she wrote on the board. *It was a dark and stormy night.*

Now, where had I heard that before?

"All you must do is think of another line that ends with a word that rhymes with *night*. And remember, class, a poem tells a story." She smiled one of her toothy smiles and stood in front of us, her long fingers locked across the front of her habit, waiting for genius to take over.

I remember the uncomfortable quiet as Sister waited...and waited...and waited. And while she waited I stared at those perfectly formed words on the blackboard. When I could bear that no longer, I stared at my best friend, Dolores, who was busy staring back at me. When my lip started to quiver in a smirk, I pressed my lips firmly together and faced forward lest Sister feel I wasn't taking poetry learning seriously.

My eyes searched the classroom for some sort of a clue—anything. I searched the fat bolts that secured my desk to the oak floorboards. I counted the shoelace holes in my gray oxford shoes. I grabbed my eraser and cleaned all the smudges off the top of my desk. Finally, when I could think of nothing else to do, I looked up again into the face of my teacher and the unusually coarse hairs that protruded from the cleft in her chin. My eyes transfixed as I counted the hairs. One...two...three.

The nun's weak voice broke the silence. "Anyone? Can anyone give me another line?"

No hands. No one spoke. We all sat with our dish plate faces and vacant stares. Finally, Sister heaved a long weary sigh. She walked to the blackboard and wrote, providing us with another line to the poem. *Filled with full moon, dark shadows, and fright.*

Determined as she was to teach us poetry, she turned back to the class, inhaled deeply, and ever so sweetly stated, "Boys and girls, we have just completed a couplet."

We? She's the one who did all the work, I thought.

"A couplet," she continued, "is made up of two rhyming lines of poetry. Notice how *night* rhymes with *fright*? Now let's continue with our spooky poem. Can anyone give me two more lines? Keep in mind they don't have to rhyme with the other two. They may be completely different. Can anyone think of two more lines for our very scary poem? Anyone?"

There was a long pause as many of us furrowed our brows and glared intently at the blackboard to let sister know we were thinking...HARD!

"Please, will anyone rise to the occasion? It's worth a star on your uniform."

"Anita? Dolores? Anthony?" she pleaded.

Suddenly, as if that Great Poet Laureate in the Sky whispered into my ear, *Put the nun out of her misery*, a thought erupted inside of me. No! Wait! Not just *one* thought, a *couplet* of thoughts. *I've got it! I've got it!* My adrenaline pumped, my pulse quickened, and my hand shot up. New hope shone across my teacher's face. She leaned towards me.

"Yes, Eileen?"

I slid out of my seat and stood, hands at my sides, my sweaty fingers pinching the pleats of my navy blue uniform. I stared into my teacher's face and blurted out,

"When suddenly I heard a whack.

It came from the railroad track!"

As if in some exotic religious ritual, Sister grasped the long string of beads that hung from her right hip and pressed the crucifix to her lips. "Praise be to Jesus, Mary, and Joseph! I think the girl has it! Eileen Farrell has it! Eileen, this is just what I want. It's perfect!" She marched over to me and affixed a tiny gold star to my uniform.

Had I heard that right? It's perfect? Had Sister Leonto said it was perfect? Every head in the room turned my way. Heat rose from my neck to my ears as the nun asked me to repeat my lines slowly while she wrote them across the chalkboard for all to admire. Her words raced through my head.

"Eileen, this is just what I want. It's perfect!"

Well, color me cool. Kids who had never bothered with me before whispered, "Wow, how did you think of that? You're so smart." Yes, I had to admit they were right.

They say that everyone experiences fifteen minutes of fame in his or her lifetime. Mine lasted throughout recess and the rest of the afternoon.

By the next day that gold star had peeled off my uniform and the other kids had already forgotten about their Fifth Grade Rhyming Queen, but I hadn't. I carried myself differently for months after that, and every time I passed Sister Leonto's desk, we exchanged smug smiles.

Thinking back to that beautiful October morning so many years ago, I realize it was because of a determined teacher's poetry lesson, and a few simple words of praise to a fifth-grade student, that I now call myself a writer.

Author Biography

Richard Knowles

Richard Knowles began writing after retiring, about six years ago. Since then he has been a winner in a number of writing contests. He is a two-time winner in both the Pamlico Writing Contest and the Carteret Writers Contest. This year he was also a winner in the Porter Fleming Literary Competition, sponsored by the Morris Museum of Art in Augusta, Georgia. Richard's favorite genres are nonfiction and fiction. He currently resides and writes on Harkers Island with his wife, Jill, and labradoodle, Rosie.

2017 Competition
Nonfiction Second Place

Alligator River Reprieve

By Richard Knowles

It was late, nearly midnight, on the third day of a nonstop journey down the Intracoastal Waterway. The ICW, a series of sounds and bays, connected by rivers and man-made canals, stretches from Boston to the southern tip of Florida, providing an inside passage for boats, a safe alternative to the open ocean. There were four of us on board *Harmony*, my 34-foot sailboat, only two of us with any sailing experience. We were moving *Harmony* from Solomons Island, Maryland, in the Chesapeake Bay, to her new home in Belhaven, North Carolina, a distance of nearly 300 miles. We had to make the trip nonstop to get it done in four days, as we all had to get back to our jobs.

We chose the Intracoastal Waterway for the trip, even though sailing offshore would have been faster, but the off-shore weather forecast suggested a pretty rough ride. With two novice sailors aboard, an ocean passage didn't seem like a prudent choice. Taking the inside route meant that we'd be motoring, not sailing, but we'd be safe and no one would be seasick. Our route had thus far brought us down the Chesapeake Bay to Norfolk Harbor, through the Dismal Swamp Canal, the Pasquotank River, and across Albemarle Sound.

As the owner and captain of the boat, I bore the responsibility for the safety of the vessel and everybody aboard. Consequently, I'd had very little sleep over the past several nights, and the trip across Albemarle Sound had been a choppy, tiring, two-hour slog. The resulting fatigue was beginning to erode my judgment and my confidence.

Leaving Albemarle Sound behind, we entered the more protected mouth of the Alligator River, but my relief at finally being out of the wind and chop was short lived. I now had a new problem. I couldn't see the opening in the drawbridge, somewhere several miles ahead. I could see the lights of cars crossing the bridge, but only faintly, and I was no longer in a marked channel. I stared ahead intently, straining to see some indication of where the opening might be in the nearly two-mile-long bridge across the upper reaches of the river. The Alligator River Bridge carries U.S. Route 64 across the river to the island of Manteo and ultimately to the popular vacation beach towns on North Carolina's Outer Banks. The highway runs east/west, the river north/south. The former runs to civilization, the latter away from it.

Unable to find the Alligator River channel markers, and worried about running aground in the shallows, I radioed the bridge tender. I hoped someone would be on duty and awake at this hour. It was, after all, a weekday night in late October. To my relief, a voice responded. When I asked where I might find the opening span in the bridge, the on-duty bridge tender replied that she didn't see any sailboats anywhere, and asked if I was sure I was calling the right bridge. This did not improve my confidence level. I told her I thought I was approaching the U.S. 64 bridge over the Alligator River - was that her bridge? "Yes," she replied, "Blink your lights so I can locate you." After doing this several times, she said "Oh, my goodness, I see you now. You need to turn hard left immediately, or you'll be aground in the marsh. I'll turn on all of my spotlights so you can see where I am."

My longtime friend Ferrand, the only other person in the cockpit at the time, said the kindest thing one can possibly say at an embarrassing moment like this: nothing at all. I motored in silence the two miles or so to the now brightly-lit opening span, muttering something like "You would think they would have it lit like this all the time."

As we passed through the now open span in the bridge and started down the river, I tried to suppress a new fear developing deep inside my psyche. The Alligator River passes through some of the wildest, least populated areas of the east coast. At the upper end, the river is several miles wide, with a well-marked channel, but as you move down the river, the channel markers become unlit day markers, and at the lower end there are no markers at all. And that name. Alligator River. Why that name? Neither Ferrand nor I spoke of any of this, of course—at least not that night.

Sitting at the helm, I listened carefully to the sound of the small diesel engine for the slightest hint of trouble, pondering what I would do if the engine stopped. I silently regretted not having refueled in Elizabeth City. *Harmony*, being a very old, vintage wooden sailboat, had no fuel gauge. She wasn't built to motor up and down the Intracoastal Waterway; she was a blue water sailing vessel.

Ferrand positioned himself at the bow, occasionally shining a light ahead, looking for obstructions. Then a minor miracle occurred. The cloud cover passed, and the sky opened up to a beautiful full moon - a bright, orange, oversized moon, lighting a path in front of us, right down the middle of the river. The river suddenly had street lights. All I had to do was drive the boat down the moonbeam. I was Dorothy in Oz, and this was the Yellow Brick Road

This slice of Nirvana lasted about an hour, and then, like the chicken that realizes the log it is sitting on seems to be moving, I noticed that the moon seemed to be moving lower in the sky – it was approaching the horizon. *Oh no, the moon is going to set. My moon is going to leave me out here, all alone again in the dark. In the middle of The Alligator River. Moon, stop! Don't do this!* But the moon turned a deaf ear, and the darkness and fear came slithering back. My mood turned once again to one of despair.

Then...darkness, pitch black. We were motoring down the Alligator River, a river with few navigation markers, full of barely submerged tree stumps, miles from civilization, alone, so totally alone. And the "what if" game began again: What if the motor quit? What if we hit something? What if we ran aground? Are there actually "alligators'" in this river? Why else would they name it the "Alligator River?" And for sure, there were snakes. Maybe pounding through ocean waves for several days wouldn't have been such a bad choice after all.

But then, once more, salvation. As the sky turned totally dark, the moon was replaced by stars. We were now under a brilliant celestial canopy. I had traded earth's moon for all of the suns of the visible universe. There were more stars in that sky, at that moment, than I had ever seen in my life. There is absolutely no artificial light in the middle of that river, once you get more than a couple of miles below the bridge. It was late October, and the sky was impossibly clear.

I handed the tiller to Ferrand and hurried below to wake the other two members of the crew, both of whom had been sound asleep since we started across Albemarle Sound. "I'm sorry, but you've got to wake up and go up on deck. There's a sight up there that you may never have a chance to see again," I proclaimed. "Trust me; it's worth it."

When we all gathered on deck, I turned off the engine and let *Harmony* drift, slowly and silently, while we all just stood staring up into the night sky. The only sounds were the gentle lapping of water moving past the boat and the occasional hooting of an owl somewhere in the surrounding forest. For what seemed like a very long time, nobody said anything, each of us alone with our thoughts. I tried hard to be mindful of the Buddhist imperative to be "in the moment." I tried to appreciate the rare glimpse of the enormity of the universe. I thought about the symbolism of four souls, adrift on a tiny boat, in a dark river, in the middle of the wilderness, under all those stars, all of those other worlds.

And what were the others thinking? Only they know, because you see, we were all guys. I imagine that if the crew on *Harmony* had been women, there would have been a great deal of discussion about the meaning of it all. But with four guys, you get insightful comments like...

"That's a hell of a lotta stars."

"Hey, isn't that the Big Dipper, right there?"

"Where are we?"

"Everybody get away from the rail, I need to pee."

And so on.

The two sleepers went back to their bunks while Ferrand and I continued the journey under the stars. The rest of the trip down the river was largely uneventful, false dawn beginning to lighten the sky as we neared the lower end of the river, where it made an abrupt turn to the right. After the turn, the river narrowed to less than 100 feet wide. According to the chart the entrance to the Pungo River Canal, the last leg of our trip, would be about three miles ahead on the left, and it would be important not to miss that entrance. Beyond the canal entrance, the river would quickly become too shallow for a boat the size of *Harmony* to navigate–we'd go aground in the river mud.

At our current speed, it would take about 30 minutes to reach the canal entrance. I sent Ferrand to the bow to scan the shoreline with binoculars, to look for some indication of an entrance to the canal. After a few minutes, he came back and said: "There's something really weird up ahead—I think you need to look at it." What I saw when I looked through the binoculars was a wall of fog, boiling up from the water, along the left shoreline, about a mile ahead. It looked like a boiling cauldron on a cold day, but I knew what I was looking at, having seen it before. The water in the narrow canal was warmer than the water in the much broader Alligator River, resulting in a concentration of fog surrounding the canal entrance. I explained all this to Ferrand, saying that it was nature's navigation gift on this fine morning, a natural marker for the entrance to the canal. Even though I understood the reason for the fog, it still felt creepy. It looked for all the world like a misty door to another world, something out of *The Mists of Avalon*. Would we pierce the fog door and enter another world? Would we just never emerge from the fog? I felt a bit of trepidation about penetrating that misty barrier, but I kept those thoughts to myself because by now all hands were on deck.

"Where are we now?"

"Who's makin' coffee?"

"Are we there yet?"

"We're about to enter the Pungo River Canal, guys – just up ahead. Then it'll be about 50 miles to Belhaven. We'll get there sometime late this afternoon," I said, ignoring the rest of it.

"The *what* canal?"

"Pungo River."

"I know what an alligator is, what's a Pungo? Or is that just a species of alligator?"

"It's the name of an old Indian Tribe."

"What's all that smoke?"

"It's not smoke, it's fog. That's where we're headed."

"Looks like a nuclear explosion to me."

"Well, it's not, it's just fog. Now quit asking me questions, I have to pay attention." In the few remaining moments, before we came abreast of the entrance, I reminded myself of an old Marine Corps saying, "Danger is inevitable, fear is optional." With that, I pushed the tiller hard over to make the turn out of the Alligator River and directly into the swirling fog portal.

Motoring through the fog turned out to be a pleasant experience, as the visibility from inside was much better than I expected. We were now a part of the misty world that we had only been able to guess about from the outside. The mist made the world look and feel softer. It took a short time to get through it and into a stretch of canal where the sun had already burned off the fog, and we were under a clear blue sky. I think we were all just a bit disappointed though that our misty ride had been so short.

In retrospect, the fears that had consumed me on the Alligator River and the Great Wall of Fog now seemed a bit foolish. Everything was going to be just fine.

We were all busy chattering about the events of the past three days, ribbing each other about all the things guys rib each other about, and then ... the silence, the deafening silence of an engine that is no longer running. *Oh, God, not now. Not less than 50 miles from our destination.*

"Hey Captain, how come the engine isn't running?"

"Uh, I think we're out of fuel, guys. Remember, we decided we didn't need to refuel in Elizabeth City? Well, maybe we should have."

"So, you have a spare fuel can ... right?"

"Uh, well, no we don't."

"So, what are we gonna do, Captain?"

"Get on the VHF radio and ask for assistance."

Which I did, and another boat coming up the canal from Belhaven responded and was tied up to our boat within a half hour. The Skipper of *Wanderer III* gave us enough diesel fuel to complete our last 50 miles safely, wished us good luck, and gently admonished me for not having an emergency container of fuel aboard.

Later that afternoon, the crew of *Harmony* sat on the lawn at the River Forest Manor and Marina, in Belhaven, drank a few beers, and re-lived the big trip. We all agreed that it had been an event to remember and that we'd have to do it again one day.   And no, nobody mentioned how much worse it would have been, had we run out of fuel in the middle of the night, amidst all those creatures, real and imagined, in the Alligator River.

Author Biography

Linda Bledsoe

Linda was born in Henry County, Virginia and raised in Virginia and North Carolina. She completed a Registered Nurse Degree and received a certificate to practice as a Family Nurse Practitioner. In Nashville Tennessee, she worked in the city's ghetto providing health care and later graduated with a BS in Liberal Arts from New York State University, than a Masters Degree in Applied Behavioral Science in Counseling Psychology from Johns Hopkins University.

While serving 33 years as a Nurse Practitioner she formulated public awareness programs for addictions and co-founded the Ecumenical Family Life Center for counseling services for abused and neglected.

She wrote and formatted a book for infertility clients, which was utilized for her teaching classes at National Naval Medical Center (NNMC) where she co-authored several research medical journal articles published in JAMA and OB-GYN.

After returning to her childhood Virginia roots, she purchased a historic home and opened Victoria's Hearth Bed & Breakfast.

She was recently awarded the first prize at the Rockingham County Fine Arts Festival for an excerpt called "Granny Isabelle and Us" from her novel "Through the Needle's Eye."

2017 Competition
Nonfiction Honorable Mention

Eighty Something

By Linda Bledsoe

My annual Asheville road trip ended at Beulah's toxin-free, off-the-grid home. My lifelong friend's abode lay nestled south-side, on the steepest mountain. Tall poplars, black pines, and bulbous oaks hovered over ancient verdant rhododendron and mountain laurel, neighbored by deer paths.

Stone Toad, a recently hauled, frog-like boulder, greeted me at the driveway. With queasy guts, I sucked in an anticipatory breath and proceeded to the house. Her urgent phone call had surged my anxiety. Was she experiencing a spiritual emergency?

Beulah—a planet cleansing Trojan, a Mother Earth warrior—now oversaw waning botanical gardens. I was saddened as I reminisced how she'd dragged heavy logs through rain or shine, building those raised vegetable plots. Hot humid compost bins perched about, crawling with massive earthworms, like anacondas. At times, hungry black bear fed from them, as if they were lifelines.

Opposites we've been forever. I grew from sticky red Virginia clay; Beulah came from Ohio's rich farm soil. Her totem was a mountain goat; her strong thick goat legs and oversized ankles had taken her many places, such as boating the Amazon River and hiking the White Mountains. My icon, a dragon fly, matched my slender well-calved legs and frame, less adept for mountains and river.

We've pushed each other's political buttons forever. She has always been a staunch Democrat. I am a Democrat, Republican, Independent, or Tea-partier if need be. My friend is for gay rights, abortion, and most things. I am anti-lots.

I'm straight Jesus. Her idols: a new goddess or guru every year, a Buddha, or some other statuette. It depends on "which book falls off of the shelf," she'd say. Why could she never be satiated and at peace with one, I'd often wondered?

A few years back, on a broiling day, we'd hightailed it to a nearby annual literary festival. "You have to come with me. The agenda is packed with famous authors," she'd wailed into the phone.

We went. Mutt and Jeff. Christopher Robin and Pooh Bear. I, in flashy bejeweled turquoise sandals, hot pink toenails, starched blouse and skinny jeans. Beulah, natural fibered, wore a long threadbare purple cotton dress layered with two sweaters, orange and lavender, wadded up posteriorly like a hot dog bun. And scruffy brown brogans with thick turned down woolen socks. To my chagrin, she sported, without apology, a faded yellow-orange knitted floppy-eared hat—designed much like those of WWII pilots.

What a site we must have been. Who knew that my friend held two distinguished master's degrees? She dawdled beside me, her green backpack full, slopping mint tea in tight Mason jars. Full-of-happy over us being together, she'd give toothy grins to passersby, never mind the basil stuck to her upper incisor. *Another memory.*

Hugging me, "My dear friend. You've made it." Her teeth, amber-hued from bottles of brown liquid cleanser, and a cartoonish grin greeted me. What happened to soda, I wondered? My tongue slithered instinctively over my oral pearls, to supernaturally whiten them.

Relieved by her young-of-heart look, luggage gathered, I followed her heels. The door opened. Sandals were offed at the threshold, as spoors of lavender, herbs, garlic, and onions pampered my nose. After settling the futon bedding, I wound downstairs and busied myself helping her.

We'd finished raspberry scones and peppermint tea, our usual "deep" conversation treat. Dark mint dregs loosened and chortled sluggishly out of the teapot, water swishing. I placed it upside down to drain beside the metal crescent-moon sieve, while Beulah wax-papered leftover biscuits.

"It's time to die soon," she said easily as if telling time. "It's why I called you." Wooden chair legs scraped linseed-coated floor, like nails on a blackboard. Her skirt tail rustled, puffing against the cane chair as she seated.

"Oh," I replied, glancing over my shoulder. Fragile dishes clinked beneath a pile of organic suds like silver pocket coins rattling.

"I want you to have that teapot set, footed sugar bowl, and matching pitcher." Her eyes bored into mine. "You know you're my best friend," she pressed. My head shook certainly.

I squirmed. "I'm trying to get rid of my own things. Give those to your kids."

"Oh, shush. Not one of them has called or come in years. Mary Jean came here some years back and stole Mama's brooch. The gold one with the pearls. She admitted it. All she had to do was ask." Beulah huffed as if it had happened yesterday. Neither of us wanted to believe those we'd given birth to could be so unscrupulous.

"Oh my, she did that?"

"I don't have anyone but you." Sadness crawled over her face, like a shadow.

A surge of annoyance arose in my chest. Yet, I understood somewhat. She'd become reclusive and her eccentricities were extreme, declaring herself allergic to all synthetic scents. Who, but me, would bathe in goat milk soap to decontaminate when visiting? I envisioned her rushing, passionately washing my night's linen, as soon as I left.

"I think it's the way the world works now. People are disjointed. They don't speak on phones. No need for a personal association. Just texting and Facebook now."

"I don't know what's happening to the world," she said, groping for answers.

"You know the library has free computer classes. You might want to try it, get linked to the outside, maybe your kids," I reminded her. "We must try to adapt to technology or we'll be left behind."

"I know. I know. Yada, yada, yada. Whatever, whatever." She shrieked. Repetition annoying me, I turned deaf ears. "I've tried the classes. I need one-on-one." She hissed. "Everything is so fast. Like the world is flying out of control. Sucked into a non-ceasing vortex."

"In ten years what will it be like?" I added.

She nodded. "Even the way people talk now. Especially the younger ones. Their words run into and all over one another. Where did diction go? God forbid spelling. I never thought it would end like this?"

"End like what?" She looked at me knowingly. I'd pulled the old psychology reflection phrase. We both had well-worn psychology degrees and still used them in personal crisis.

"Be alone with—" she stalled, "without anyone to lean on. I have kids, yet, I really don't."

"You were a good mother and still are."

"I was a good mother. I baked pies, cakes, and bread from scratch. I washed their clothes and read them stories. They never got over the divorce. Everyone thought I should have stayed with him. God forbid, he was a preacher of a big church. Can you imagine?" She paused. "Why would anyone stay with a drunk batterer?" Her hand searched and smothered her chest as if her heart ached.

"Only two people stuck by you, right?" I'd heard it all before.

"That's right. Out of a thousand members, only two. He was a closet drinker. Said he had rights to my body any time he wanted. Didn't I tell you that?" She had. "Even the deacons wouldn't listen. After I left, he was with some floozy within six weeks. Met her at a preacher's convention in Chicago." Jowls dropped, as disgust groped her face.

I gulped. "I guess people don't want to believe their leader isn't perfect. I know it had to be awful," I tendered, thinking spiritual murder is the worst kind. Helpless, I shrugged without answers for her unjustified loneliness. Knowing people often seek homeostasis and side with the manipulator, the abuser, in these situations.

Her life's work as a therapist had never made her own pain go away. I looked at her positive Post-it notes stuck around the kitchen. "Let go and let live." Live in the moment. Be all that you can. " She'd stuffed positivity into my life. I too had reminders throughout my home, bowls of sweet lavender and sage scattered about, warding off evil spirits.

She, my quirky pal, always in my corner, through many cruel life ordeals. She thought I could move mountains, and I did. But she moved many more. She created great "camps" for the hurting, called "Healing the Child." One camp collected professionals of all kinds: psychiatrists, psychologists, doctors, and lawyers came to her to work on their inner child. We operated as a team, on ourselves and on others as if we were psychological surgeons.

Later, after our feast, we hiked a bit, Beulah climbing easily as I trudged uphill panting. Shuffling, she squatted beneath a great hemlock, gently caressing the dead leaves. "It's my grave," she said. "I want you to know where it is." I gasped, gazing at the earthy rectangle. "The dirt will be softened, not so hard to dig. There will be no casket. I want my bones to go back to Mother Earth like they're meant to."

"Why are we talking about this now?" I groaned.

"Because you need to make sure it's like I want. No big deal. Just letting go."

"Letting go of what? You've still got a lotta spunk. Climb like a mountain goat."

She eyed me. "Just wrap me in Mama's quilt. The worn out one in the cedar chest. The one I showed you last year. You remember. It'll be just fine."

A new grief awakened and ripped my core. Not only was she aging, so was I. Here we stood together, facing our mortality on Billy Goat Hill.

"I don't want IV's, tubes running in and out of me. No nursing homes. No hospice."

"And if your kids want otherwise," I plied.

Glossing over my question, she said, "It's like my Frasier friends in New York. Marie's husband, David, said when he couldn't chop his wood, he was ready to go to the other side. He went away when he was 102. Marie died a few weeks later in an accident." Her fingers quoted accident. "When I go, it'll be like David. I'll just lie down, quit eating and drinking. I've made my mind up." Her eyes pled with mine. "I don't want doctors and hospitals keeping me alive when nothing's left for me to do."

I nodded. "You certain?"

"Never more positive over anything in my life. Read that piece from Mary Oliver, 'The Journey.' Then I'll take off and do a new thing." Tears trolled downward. "And put my floppy-eared cap on me." She squawked.

Our laughter soared, honking like Canada geese. Youthful vigor chortled within as we rejoiced over past voyages. Climbing mountains, crossing rocky streams with moleskin laden heel-blisters, sailing with Washington Women Outdoors on the Chesapeake, rock climbing, and biking through Washington's parks.

Beulah put the kettle on when we returned. Steam spurted. "All of those precious things don't mean much anymore. China teacups, sugar bowls, and creamers with legs, gold brooches, and silver spoons. What means the most to me are memories of our healing camps, those people recovering from lost childhoods, finding their inner-selves. Remember that book by Charles Wingfield, *Healing the Inner Child*? Best book ever wrote." Thought-sated, she smacked her lips. "Would you like another cup of tea and a raspberry scone?" She asked.

"Believe I will. So, what's next? Since you have all these dark issues cleared away."

Eyes sparkled. "Well, I am leaving Wednesday."

"Oh, where might you be off this time, since you're not ready for dying today?"

"Going hang gliding. Always wanted to. Not putting it off. No time to waste. It's my birthday present to myself."

"And how old are you?" I said as she unwrapped a new sweater I had for her.

"Oh, eighty something."

We unwrapped the warmed scones. Sipping, chewing, smacking lips in unison, as the moon's perky glow twinkled on our china cups. Again, we reviewed all the delicious details of our experiences that grew us up into real women. Remember when....

Author Biography

Deborah Doolittle

Deborah has lived in lots of different places but now calls North Carolina home. She has a B.A. from the University of Colorado, an M.A. from George Washington University, an M.F.A. from San Diego State University, and now teaches at Coastal Carolina Community College. Two chapbooks, *No Crazy Notions,* and *That Echo* have won the Mary Belle Campbell and Long Leaf Press Award, respectively. She has had more than 350 poems published in literary magazines, with some most recently having appeared or will soon appear in *Atlanta Review, Bear Creek Haiku, Edge, Oberon, Pinyon, Seems,* and *TAB: The Journal of Poetry and Poetics.* An avid print-maker, she has put together a small collection of handmade limited edition book art. Married to a retired Marine, she has a son and a daughter and three grandchildren. When not teaching or writing, she volunteers as a Wildlife Rehabilitator. She and her husband currently share their house with four cats and a backyard full of birds.

2017 Competition
Poetry First Place

Self-Portrait, Swimming

By Deborah Doolittle

Try hard not to count each stroke, each time
my fingers slip beneath the water's

surface, each kick that breaks into air
inadvertently. Each gulp of pure

oxygen will suffice. Lips pulled in
a smooth round "O." Just how goldfish

kiss the walls of an aquarium.
Head and shoulders submerged on each small

angled dive, I blow a rivulet
of bubbles behind me. My mermaid self

swims underneath on the pale blue floor,
looking more graceful then than I can

imagine I'll ever be on this
other not quite bottomless sky.

Effortlessly, breathlessly. We're both
buoyant. We palm the wall, flip and kick

back down the lane, matching one stroke to
one breath all the way. I keep the count,

much like with sheep when falling asleep.
Bleary-eyed, goggles pressed to the soft

flesh of my cheeks, we seek reflections,
trailing and dissolving in my wake.

Author Biography

Jo Ann Hoffman

Jo Ann Steger Hoffman is a writer, editor, and former corporate communications director whose publications include a children's book, short fiction and a variety of poems in literary journals, including *The Merton Quarterly, Pinesong, Fall Lines* and *New Verse News*. She has received recent contest awards from the Pamlico Writers' Group and the Palm Beach Poetry Festival. Her 2010 non-fiction book, *Angels Wear Black,* recounts the only technology executive kidnapping to occur in California's Silicon Valley. A native of Toledo, Ohio, she and her husband now live in Cary and Beaufort, North Carolina.

2017 Competition
Poetry Second Place

Love in the Long Term

By JoAnn Hoffman

We go to bed with the salt taste
of argument still on our tongues.
It comes to me at 4:00 a.m.
with the hall clock chiming
like a drumroll:
the perfect retort,
the supreme smart remark,
the ultimate zinger,
the *ha-ha-ha,*
in-your-face,
gotcha-now,
proves-you-wrong,
reply.

I punch my pillow
with smug satisfaction,
turn away from the weight
of your sleep
and curl into the comfort
of the last word,
warmed by the thought of sending
my sally smack into
your righteous self.

While the clock chimes five,
I lie listening to the rhythm
of your breath,
the soothing little *pfewts* of air
you send riding on the night.
I back up to your back.

Six chimes. Still drifting in half-sleep,
I feel your foot across my line, and find
I've rolled onto your pillow.
In this snug zone of doze and dream
my burning words dissolve in smoke.

I can't even resurrect the ashes.
In the quiet blessing of slow light,
I look at you and wonder why it ever mattered.

Author Biography

Pam Desloges

Pam grew up in the mountains of New Hampshire and spent much time on the rugged coast of Maine. After retiring from a small New England college, she lost interest in shoveling snow. She now lives in New Bern, North Carolina, with her husband, Max. She has been published in the anthology *Art Inspires Poetry*, the blog *Polly's Tea Kettle*, and a magazine for dog lovers, *Sniff & Barkens*. She is a member of the North Carolina Writers Network, the Pamlico Writer's Group, and is a founding member of the Neuse River Writers' Group.

Find her work at: https://www.facebook.com/pamdesloges

2017 Competition
Poetry Honorable Mention

Whisper of God

By Pamela Desloges

When your eye was held
by the bright blue bird
in brown dead branches

and you forgot
the car, the steering wheel
for the beauty of a bird

in an eternity
of landscape unfolding
past the open window
too quick to be real

dreamlike;
roused from bucolic slumber
to the sting of awareness,
the curve of the dusty road
leering at your carelessness

as tires bounce, spray gravel,
fender grazes pasture fence
and you adjust instinctively
not oversteering, but barely,

like avoiding your ex-husand
at a party with his new love
not wanting to shift the universe
but only survive

barely braking
cool and confident
like leaving the party
with your coat slung casually over your arm

and back on the road
bird left behind
blue still in your eyes
that are moist with fear
and
gratitude.

Author Biography

Emani Dunning

Hello, my name is Emani Dunning and I am 18 years old. I am from Greenville, NC, where I attended and recently graduated from South Central High School. I love to spend time with my family and friends, eat, help others and smile! I am now a freshman at Winston-Salem State University with a major in Biology, to have a successful career as a neonatologist or pediatrician and with writing being something I do well, I also plan to become an author. I would like to thank my supportive family, and Mrs. Painter for giving me this opportunity, and also the Pamlico Writers for granting me this title! God bless!

2017 Competition
High School First Place Prose

Katherine

By Emani Dunning

We waited patiently, looking everywhere but each other's eyes. We didn't dare to make eye contact for we knew that if we did, it would only be a river of tears. I couldn't hold it in anymore, tears streamed down my face and the saltiness of them reached my lips.

"Lauren?" someone said. I looked up, feeling the stares of the rest of my family all upon me.

"I just need some air," I replied. I got up and walked out of the family sitting room. My mind was full, I thought of everything as I made my way to the elevator. I couldn't keep my thoughts inside and before I knew it, they came rushing out of my mouth. *"Why is this happening to me? To us? To her? Where is this God that everyone speaks of that heals and delivers?"* The elevator came to a stop. I eased my way through the crowd of people, trying to get away from the faint smell of disinfectant and that awful stuff they call food. I glanced around, some individuals and some families all looking frantic or tired or both. They smelled as if they had been there for days. Ugh! I got to the entrance, and that's when the flashbacks hit me.

I was sitting in the front row of the pews, watching every person that passed. Elder women approached my siblings and me, repeating the same phrase as the person before them as if they recited it. "Everything is going to be okay, call me if you need anything." Or "She's in a better place, God is with her." I zoned out, only taking notice of the strong, nose-wrenching perfume every other lady had on as they brushed past me with their wide hats and their fascinators covering their faces.

I drifted in and out of the service, the dirges the only thing sticking in my memory. The speaker of the service who appeared to be omniscient was discursive with his sermon, his words making me feel uneasy. I was hot, steaming it felt like, as beads of sweat started to form on my forehead. The gloves I wore were sticking to my hands, becoming increasingly irritating. I glanced at my brother and my sister, both of them looking miserable. I looked down at my ruffled socks sticking out of from my "good church shoes" as my grandmother would say. At that moment, it all came crashing down on me. I was alone—we were alone. We had nobody. Our mother was gone and all that existed of her now was a cold figure lying in a casket.

My siblings and I were only kids, my brother and I not yet teenagers. How were we supposed to take care of ourselves? When the phone calls stop, and the people stop coming and the different dishes which everyone had brought were all devoured, what would happen? Surely my siblings hadn't thought of this, as I was considered to overthink too much and stress before there was even anything to stress about. Our mom was dead, and all we could do was cry the tears we couldn't stop from flowing, in hopes that they would bring her back to us.

My eyes drifted shut, and I was awakened by my brother pulling at my arm, announcing it was time to go...the funeral was over. We got into the funeral car, the silence and heavy breathing carrying us until we got to the cemetery. Moments passed and I'm not sure if I was in my right state of mind or not. Before I knew it, the casket was being lowered into the ground. My heart sank. My breath quickened. The tears were endless. I had lost my everything, I had lost my heart. My mom was gone.

I came to, finding myself still standing at the entrance. "Excuse me, are you lost?" someone asked. I looked up and it was one of the clerks from the front desk.

"No, I'm not," I replied. "I'm here for a family member." The clerk asked me for a name. "Katherine.... Katherine Miles." The clerk looked up the name and handed me a sticker. "Room 301, east wing." I walked off, threw the sticker away, and headed back to the room. I made my way back to the family room and saw my family sitting where I had left them. They looked up at me upon my arrival, all of their faces portraying different emotions. I took my seat in a corner by myself. I didn't want to be bothered. I was torn down on the inside, my heart aching. But I feigned that I was okay. We had been here a total of nine hours. I remember it so well, something I don't think I'll ever forget. My grandmother had been in so much pain, I went to her bedroom hearing the faint cries she happened to make, only to find layers of her flesh spread over the bed sheet. I didn't know what to say or do, so I made my way to the front room and stayed there watching each of my family members make their way in. I made eye contact with my cousin, her eyes full of terror. I could tell she and I were thinking the same thing: our grandmother had been in stage four skin cancer longer than we knew. We only found out recently, when our parents told us she didn't have much time to live. It was all new information, like a slap in the face. We didn't know how to take it. All I knew was that I had to be strong for my cousin while trying to muster up strength for myself.

Now here we are. Our grandmother, mother, wife, sister...could be well or could be taking her last breath. *"Another loss, another funeral,"* I thought to myself. I can't take it. I start to look around, my legs shaking frantically. My mouth is dry and my fingernails are only nubs now. I'm about to let out the tears I've been trying to hold in when the doctor comes to the door.

"Family of Katherine Miles?" We all stood up at once, my family looking directly at the doctor, or staring at the floor. My aunt was playing with her rings on her fingers. My grandfather had his eyes closed, and I knew that he was praying. My dad and I were the only ones making eye contact, for he knew what I had been thinking this whole time. Neither one of us took death well and with all of the deaths on my father's side of the family, he'd only attended one funeral. It seemed as if we were waiting for years; I could hear the ticking of the clock. I broke the stare between my father and me and looked at the doctor.

"I'm very sorry, but she didn't make it."

My thoughts went back to the days we would cook in the kitchen, the long hours we spent at church that my cousin and I would complain of. The late nights our grandmother would stay up with us and me....I thought about the times I saw her smile and the secrets we kept that we promised to take to our grave. It was all over. Those days were gone. As tears rolled down my face, I looked at my phone for the time. It was 12:23 a.m. February 14th. Valentine's Day. A day meant for love and happiness, and I had lost my most cherished loved one.

Author Biography

Natalie Valentine

Natalie Pauline Valentine was born in San Jose, California, and her family now currently resides in Greenville, North Carolina.

She is a senior in High School and is currently attending the University of North Carolina School of the Arts in the High School Program, studying Drama. Aside from writing and acting, she is an alumna of the Outdoor Academy and loves backpacking, rock climbing, and canoeing.

She hopes to attend college to receive her degree in acting, and to go on to be a professional actress. Her dream is to perform at the Royal Shakespeare Company. She hopes to continue writing while she pursues her acting career.

2017 Competition
High School First Place Poetry

the girl who wanted to be friends with the moon (and the stars and the planets)

By *Natalie Valentine*

a pale baby girl
arrived into the world on a rainy tuesday afternoon
and became the unknowing hostage
of a tormented home.
she was a surprise, the unplanned third;
an accident, a soul forged from the longing pale moonlight
instead of the sunny love of glowing from her parents.
she learned to grow up lonely;
a scrappy little weed of a girl;
her friends were books, the firefly fairies in the garden
that only came out at night.
(they hid from her, but loved her so.)
she told herself stories
loved playing pretend
in her cramped little room with a sheer canopy
(pink like a tutu, one that a ballerina wears)
that she would draw around her like a cocoon
and fill her bed with books borrowed from the library
about space and rockets and solar systems.
she liked imagining a house full of jolly people
cheerful and inviting, with baking cookies and fresh flowers in
vases,
while the screaming battles
raged on, just on the other side of her bedroom door.
her room was her burrow, a little hole to hide
from the tempestuous screaming storm swirling outside
(complete with glowing stickers of stars of the ceiling).
her family was broken,
but she became whole
by watching the stars and drawing pictures of the constellations
in a torn little notebook she kept under a rock

and leaving presents for the fairies.
and, at night, she would tuck each doll into bed, giving them all
equal love
(even though the blue-eyed baby was her favorite)
afraid her toys would feel just as alone
as she did on the nights
sitting in her room
hiding from the formidable chilling silence that made her tummy
feel like
stone. (tread carefully little one)
she took to calling on her friends
the whirlpool of stars and planets and moons
the ones she watched so fondly
to take her in their incandescent ghostly arms
and cradle her like a newly born child.
to whisper of love and hope and god and pennies and
candy and books and chalk
and christmas lights and white horses and tea
and pain and plums and polka dots
and stubbed toes and sunburns.
because what she craved with the longing
of a cooing mourning dove
on a dewy mountain morning
were stories of her own to share
and a darling companion to hear them.
(please find her soon)

Monthly 1,000 Word Challenge

One of the 2017 Pamlico Writers' Group initiatives to encourage writing is the monthly writing challenge. A picture prompt with short text description is offered. Participants are asked to write a fiction work within the 1,000-word limit. Monthly winners have been chosen with their reward being the publication of their works that follow.

Author Biography

Sherri Hollister

Sherri Lupton Hollister is the recent chairperson for the Pamlico Writer's Group. She loves everything about writing from the first glimmer of an idea to the final product. Reading, reviewing, discussing and learning about other writers and their process has helped develop her own writing. Sherri writes romantic suspense set in a small Southern town.

She lives with her own romantic hero, her husband of more than 25 years. Together they raised six sons and will soon welcome their eighteenth grandchild. Sherri hopes to publish the first book in her series, *Chrome Pink,* this spring.

April Writer's Challenge

What would your character do? Commit murder? Take their life? Write in 1000 words or less and tell us how the story ends.

Six Bullets

By Sherri Hollister

The glow of the brass and copper in the flicker of the candlelight blurred with the flow of her tears. The cool metal warmed in the palm of her hand. Silently she counted each bullet as she loaded the revolver her father had left her. One, two...the third rolled to the floor. Her heart pounded. She glanced at the door, swallowing the pool of saliva that gathered in her mouth. Her hands shook. She forced herself to stay on task. She inserted number four in the cylinder. Her fingers, slick from perspiration, fumbled five and six. They rolled under the kitchen table. Exhaling, she shuddered and took a deep breath. Her blood felt like a tidal wave in her ears. She scooted to the edge of the vinyl seat. Gripping the aluminum leg of the scarred Formica table, she searched for the stray bullets.

The candle's light didn't reach the shadows beneath the table. Unable to afford to keep it on, she'd had the electricity turned off after the funeral. Her body protested as she eased to the cold floor.

Every muscle ached, the cut on her knee burned. Her lips were dry and she couldn't breathe through her nose. Every breath was labored, and she was sure her ribs were cracked if not broken. Tears slid down her bruised cheeks cooling her fevered skin. She patted the grit-coated floor searching blindly for the missing bullets. One, two, she shoved them into the chambers. She patted the cracked linoleum for the last bullet. A crunch on the gravel path stilled her hands. She gripped the revolver and held her breath.

A cold wind snuffed out the candle, plunging her into complete darkness. There is nothing so dark as a house in the country with not even a security light left on. She bit her lips to keep from crying out. The darkness threatened to smother her. She hated the dark. Bad things happen in the dark. She held the gun, trying to remember what her father taught her. She eased her grip, keeping the other hand on her wrist to steady the gun. She prayed five bullets would be enough.

"Melissa, where are you?" The sing-song voice teased.

The heavy thud of two-hundred pounds encased in heavy leather motorcycle boots shook the old house. She could feel each step through the floor joist.

"I knew you'd come running home. You're so predictable."

Where else could I go after what you did?

"Too bad Daddy isn't here to protect you." He laughed.

Melissa bit back a sob. She was sure he'd killed her father. *If only I could prove it.*

"Melissa, don't make me tear this house apart. Enough games, get out here now!"

The sudden glare of a flashlight blinded her. She pulled the trigger.

John cursed and dropped the light. It rolled beneath the table. He leaned down to pick it up, she could see his silhouette limed by the fallen flashlight. She pulled the trigger, emptying the gun. He fell. His head, what was left of it, lay shattered at her feet. Melissa pulled her feet to her and wrapped her arms around her shins. She squeezed into a tight ball. The flashlight beam glowed against the faded wallpaper leaving the gory details of John's injuries to her imagination.

She could feel the blood cooling in her canvas tennis shoes but she couldn't move. Melissa sat beneath the table where she and her father had taken all of their meals since her mother's passing. Neither of them had had any desire to sit in the formal dining room. The dining room had been her mother's pride. They'd used it for every holiday, Sunday dinner and special occasion. Any excuse her mother could find to decorate and to display her fine china. The kitchen table was her and her father's sanctuary. Here they had their discussions about life and history and books they'd read. It was their sanctuary no longer. She blinked back tears. The coppery smell of blood and the acrid scent of gunpowder permeated the air, making it hard to breathe. The cold air was heavy with the threat of rain.

"Oh my God, what happened here?"

The muffled words penetrated the fog clouding her brain. Melissa looked up into the concerned face of Sheriff Knowles. She'd known him since she was a little girl. He'd been her daddy's best friend. Sobbing, she crawled from beneath the table and threw herself against him.

The sheriff held her and shouted orders. Melissa wasn't sure if she'd lost her hearing due to shooting the gun under the table or if she was in shock and not comprehending what was being said.

Paramedics came in and eased her onto a stretcher. She clung to the sheriff's hand.

"I'll be along in a few minutes, Melissa. It's okay. You'll be safe."

She looked from the female to the male paramedics. They looked familiar but she couldn't recall their names. The woman touched her hand. "We'll take good care of you. Bixby's okay for a dude."

Melissa blinked her eyes to let her know she understood.

The sheriff's foot slipped. His black shoe sliding over the floor nearly out from under him. He caught his balance and bent down to retrieve a stray bullet.

"Number six," she whispered as the gurney was pushed from the house.

Author Biography

Michael Worthington

Michael retired after teaching college for 30 years, during which time he had published articles in trade magazines during the summers. Now he devotes his time to writing young adult novellas and volunteering in schools. Often his pug sleeps on the recliner's footrest while he types away on his laptop.

May Writer's Challenge

The night is still young. Will it be a night of romance or a night of intrigue? Only your character will know. Will you paint their path, or will they lead you by the hand?

Vacation from Hell

By Michael Worthington

Sue wondered if she dared take off her bikini top while her husband and kids were out on the lake. Lying on the elevated deck, she would have time to cover up once she heard the boat motor, unless she fell asleep. Then she had a vision of herself wearing a loose mumu to protect a painful sunburn in a most sensitive area and decided against it.

Soffie the poodle began furiously barking, so Sue got up to check on her. The vacation cottage was perched on stilts, half on land and half in the shallows with no nearby neighbors, but kids sometimes paddled canoes along the shore. Suddenly the barks morphed into frightened yips, and Sue could hear a commotion on the landing. She walked swiftly towards the stairs, planning to give those kids a piece of her mind.

Soffie reached the top of the stairs before Sue, trembling and whining in fear. It sounded like the kids were beating on the stair rails with their paddles, but Sue froze when she saw what was actually causing the commotion.

A ten-foot alligator was making its slow way up the stairs after the dog. Its body contorted into curves, first one way and then the other, as its stubby legs pushed against the uprights that supported the handrail. Some of the supports had splintered under the assault, but enough remained for the monster to pull its body fully up on the stairs, with only the tip of its tail still lying on the landing. Its gaping mouth displayed rows of sharp teeth as it relentlessly pursued its intended meal.

Sue scooped up Soffie and ran to the sliding glass door. She locked the door behind her, wondering what good that did since the reptile couldn't reach the latch anyway. Still, she retreated from the door, expecting at any moment to see that maw of ivory through the glass. She hoped that the alligator would give up once it was thwarted by the door, and slide under the banisters at the edge of the deck to dive back into the dark water below.

When the tip of the snout became visible through the door, she moved behind the counter, as if that flimsy barrier would offer more protection. Fascinated, she stared at the creature's head swinging back and forth as it steadily forced its way up the steps; more and more of the gaping jaws came into sight as it relentlessly heaved its heavy body upward.

With its front legs on the deck outside the door, the creature turned its head from side to side as if searching for its prey. Then it seemed to catch sight of the woman and dog through the door and slammed its snout against the glass. Momentarily stymied, the alligator seemed to pause to think about the situation. Then it suddenly lunged forward, shattering the glass and forcing its way into the cottage.

Frantically, Sue searched for some weapon to protect herself and her pet. She found a few long butcher knives and a meat cleaver, which all seemed pathetically useless when measured against the monster making its slow way through the door.

As it got its front feet within the doorway, Sue ran down the hall to the bathroom, locking the door behind her. She listened with growing dread to the sounds of mayhem in the main room. Then she heard the creature's claws scraping against the narrow hallway walls.

Her phone lay on the deck beside her lounge, but even if she had reached someone, they couldn't have come fast enough to save her. She opened the window and screamed for help, knowing at the time that nobody was close enough to hear her. But the fear so strongly welled up inside her, that if she didn't scream her chest would have burst.

Sue could feel the dog's pee running down her legs as she hugged it close. The poor dog whimpered in fear, whether because of its near brush with death, or just feeding off the fear of its mistress, or because Sue was squeezing the dog so hard that it had to struggle to breathe.

The scraping sounds grew louder as the beast made its way down the hall. Sue stood on her tiptoes and held the dog out the window. As she dropped Soffie, she hoped that the water would cushion the twelve-foot fall and that no other alligators waited below for a snack to drop into the water.

The noise seemed right outside the door as Sue pulled herself up into the window. She could just get her head and one arm out. Her top ripped, exposing her in a parody of her daydream of topless sunbathing. Blood trickled down her breasts as she struggled to pull her body through the tiny window. Finally, she forced her upper body through the opening, hanging in an awkward position with her hips still inside.

The door splintered, and with an adrenaline-fueled effort, she ripped the window frame out and found herself dangling upside down with one leg still caught in the opening. The noise inside grew louder as she heard the porcelain toilet shatter. The pain in her leg was excruciating; she felt the bone break as it bent at an unnatural angle; she plunged headfirst into the brown water.

The water was just deep enough to cover her bare breasts as she stood on one leg. The dog was nearby, paddling to shore. Then she heard the outboard motor, which set off new alarms in her head. Would the children run into the cabin and encounter the monster?

Frantically she swam around towards the front of the cottage to intercept her family. When they came into sight, she held her arms up and waved, sliding under the water in her effort. But she persisted until strong arms grabbed her and pulled her into the boat.

Author Biography

Janine Sellers

Janine Sellers, homemaker, wife, and daughter in a historic section of New Bern, has been writing poetry since she was sixteen.

With wordsmithing as part of her DNA, she has been the editor and cover designer of two successfully published books. The portals to Janine's world include bookstores, libraries and yard sales. She loves people, especially first-person storytellers. An excessive note-taker and memoirist, Janine strongly believes in getting things down on paper.

She is happily retired from a professional career in association management.

The Diving Bell Hotel

By Janine Sellers

You'd never know it. Sure, it looks like a fishing lodge but it's a hotel. This is Sue's sixth stay. She takes a deep breath as she moors the skiff and hops onto the dock.

"Back again, Sue! Good to see you, old friend!"

She is met by Eddy Yuber, the proprietor. The popular place is booked year round with writers who return in flocks. They've pretty much filled his calendar since he opened it eleven years ago. Poets and writers come for conferences or to write on their own. Eddy is from New York, retired IT, happy to be settled in Eastern North Carolina. He pampers guests with fresh-pressed coffee and decadent pecan coffee cake from a local bakery which he pairs with his signature bowls of local blueberries placed on tables and in guestrooms where tiny refrigerators are stocked with specialty cheeses. The kitchen is rarely used for cooking, except on Friday for the fish fry.

Sue is back for a final test of the integrity and safety of her diving bell and its long-anticipated patent. She settles onto a bar stool beside the door to the kitchen. Eddy is busy making repairs to the wrap-around dock. A gust of wind causes the door to pop, then sets the rocker outside into motion. It startles her, as she thinks about the integrity of the bell, the thickness of the wall, its balance of air pressure. Of course, it cannot crack. It is perfect. She has been tinkering with the design for seven years. Its method is simple: to allow people a limit of fourteen minutes underwater suspended nine feet under. Scuba divers wearing wetsuits and saddled with air tanks, the types who venture a half mile down—these are a different sort. At only two pounds and the size of a large kitchen trash can, it is comfortable enough for a child to wear. Sue's diving bell is skinny on space and big on "taste." Everyone who has tried it loves it, for it challenges their imagination by a process she calls *subtraction*.

She will meet with the crew for the final test at four o'clock. Danny, Maxine, and Jerry from the nearby dive shop are experienced, professional divers. Jim and Brody are engineers; Jim's with Carolina Aquarium and Brody is a Navy specialist known around the world as *the* expert in traditional diving bells. Sue's design is appropriate even for non-swimmers who want to experience the deep. A microphone keeps the one in the diving bell connected to people in the vessel above so they can communicate. Most who experience it describes the bell as exciting though it offers minimal access to the ocean floor and cannot be used in these somewhat murky waters to see much of anything. People still love it; the deprivation is medicinal. The sense you get of quiet and otherworldliness pares down to an essence, like poetry, where the process of subtraction provides peace, where for a time you have no possessions and you haven't a sense of now, then, or tomorrow.

Sue Nordstrom and her mini diving bell have received the attention of scientists, corporations, universities, sociologists, and both the conventional and unconventional. She plans to use future grant monies to offer the diving bell to PTS survivors, the disabled, even children with autism. Deprivation is healing. She knows that.

There is a small sound at the door. Steven steps in. Her ex-lover! Of course, there was always that chance they would send Steven in place of Brody Baughman. Sue and Steven had a brief, steamy affair on her second visit to the lodge, right before Eddy renamed it The Diving Bell Hotel.

Now what?

Used to be, cars were made with moving parts and men (it was mostly men) could tinker with them. Now, it is more, and less, complex, with computers analyzing what can the matter be — the car is making a small noise. Used to be, she was dumbfounded by her emotions. Today is different. She finds he shows up in her dreams, though she can control her thoughts. After tinkering with the diving bell for over seven years, she knows to keep her mind sharp, her fingers moist, to wrap her head in a towel to stay warm, to wear a hat to blanket her head from the cold or protect it from the sun.

She takes her time. She moves in his direction, anchors on his pool-blue eyes. The emotion does not wash over as before. She steadies, balances her thoughts on how to deal with the moisture on the inside of the window of the diving bell.

Sue approaches life and love with simple instructions like the How to Wash Your Hands sign in the public restroom. Use Hot Water and Soap. The feelings are familiar. She pauses, takes a travel napkin from her purse, tears open the package and after a few seconds drops the moist towelette into his outreached hand. She turns away after a lukewarm hello, and he manages to say, "Congratulations, Sue."

What was it like, the first time in the diving bell, its stillness, breathing in pumped-in air? She used to have to separate her emotions like peeling leeches from the soft skin of her belly. She remembers the time she was stung by jellyfish. How she wished upon him the torment of a thousand stings.

The mark that remains of their forbidden romance made her care more, made her more careful. It took a secret life in her brain like a fat bumblebee living off every flower in the garden. Now, she sees more flowers. Throbbing colors. Live flowers! Now, she sees all that is familiar with a new set of lenses. Today, when, by chance, they meet, she has a thousand wishes. The wishes fall to the ground and melt like snowflakes on the warm deck surrounding the hotel that seems to float in the harbor.

Author Biography

Katirie Leach

Katirie Leach is a native of Tarboro, North Carolina. She moved to Washington in 1996 when she married her husband, Jim, who is a lifelong resident. She has indulged her love of writing and painting through various endeavors in the local community.

The Water House

By Katirie Leach

He felt the rail. Splinters. There had always been splinters. Pick up your foot. Pick up your hand. Slowly he climbed up the steps from the water.

He felt the house sway, inhaling, exhaling the evening air. He heard the water lap at the pilings. He saw the purple sky fold into the mauve sea. Dusk confused him now.

He walked through the house. He could see little. Indigo light played through the windows. There was no electricity. There had never been. He returned to the back porch.He sat in the rocking chair, the only chair left.

It grew dark. Water and sky became one. The stars would come later.

His grandfather built the house. Big Daddy made a living on the water. He was a commercial fisherman but he came here to the water house to relax...and fish some more. Big Daddy brought him on his thirteenth birthday. Only men could come to the water house. It was a proud day.

He came with his father. He came with his brothers. He brought his sons when they turned thirteen. He brought his grandsons when they became men. The water house was a rite of passage...a bridge to manhood.

He smelled the fish frying. He heard the oil popping. He tasted the fish. He saw the old stove. It was wood burning. The men cut the wood and rowed it in boats to the water house. He saw the rusted icebox. He felt the cold ice as he filled Big Daddy's bourbon glass.

He heard T. Boy's banjo. He heard Cody G.'s harmonica. He heard Wilbur and Nathan's soft duets float out across the still blue water.

He saw Big Daddy with old Simon Miller, Mr. Fiddler, J.J. Wright, Slim McKinney sitting at the table playing poker by the kerosene lantern. He saw the wooden matches used as chips. He saw the bottle of bourbon and half-filled glasses.

He saw the cleaning table on the porch piled high with fish. He saw the blood, bones, heads of fish that had been swimming only hours earlier. He saw his sons hanging over the deck lowering fish heads tied to string into the blue-green water. He heard their laughter.

He rocked, he saw, he slept. Dawn's pale rose hue lined the horizon. He awoke. He rose stiffly from his chair. He looked over the still water. He sighed.

He moved towards the steps. He felt the rail. Splinters. There had always been splinters. Put down your hand. Put down your foot. Slowly he stepped down the stairs to the water.

He stepped into the boat. He started the outboard motor. He untied the line from the water house. He sat down. He put the engine in gear and turned toward the shore. Dawn had lightened the blue of the water.

He looked back. The water house floated on steel blue water. It would soon be demolished...spanned by a bridge of concrete and blue steel.

Author Biography

Gloria Loftin

I have been writing since I was five years old. That is my first love. I am also a voracious reader. I live in Grimesland, North Carolina. We moved here in 2005 from Northern Virginia. I missed out on college when I was younger. My parents had four children to support. My parents could not afford to send me to college at that time.

I had my chance when I asked my mom and dad if they would pay for me to go to college at the age of 6, and they said yes. I missed out when I was younger, but I believe that I appreciated it more at that age. Now I just love to learn, something I did not care for as a teenager.

I am unpublished but hope to remedy that soon. I have found a wonderful group of people who support and encourage every chance they get.

Thank you for the time to get to know me a little better.

June Writer's Challenge

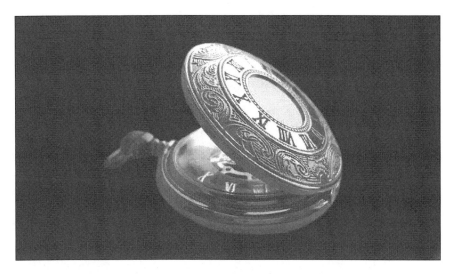

Father time waits for no one. What will your story uncover? Evidence from a crime scene? Time travel? Keepsake? Missing link to a coded message? The second hand is moving one click at a time.

Tick Tock

By Gloria Loftin

The night, midnight black with rain falling in a torrential downpour; the brick paths running red with flowing mud; the pine trees leaning, almost breaking in the violent winds. The prison almost glowing with an unnatural light, every inmate looking like a character from a horror movie starring from a hundred windows in the prison's walls.

The ancient musty prison bus, battered by the unnatural wind, is being loaded with the dregs of humanity—saved at the last minute from death. They are on their last trip to a new maximum security prison.

"tic, tock" Hardened beyond his years, the youngest of them had the face of an angel but the eyes of a stone-cold killer—condemned to die for the murder of his whole family.

"tic, tock" The oldest among them, eyes gone blank with the years of time, unable to remember what he was sentenced for, sat in silence.

"tic, tock" Bodies shifting back and forth, mucus from their noses running down their chins, idiots not caring what is in store for them—just another stark gray prison, in another dust belt town, along another black highway.

"tic, tock" Two world-weary guards and the driver sit in the front of the bus behind a gray steel cage.

"tic, tock" The prisoners sit on rusty, creaky benches on each side of the bus, chained to the floor like men on a slave ship—no hope, only death ahead.

"tic, tock" Down that black highway the bus rolls. The air outside the bus is mud-colored and hot beyond bearing.

"tic, tock" The men on the bus began to shift around and mumble under their breaths.

"Tic, Tock" You can feel their fear, their rage begin to build as they travel further, down the red, hot pavement.

"Tic, Tock" The air turns dark grey like an ominous storm-tossed sea.

"Tic Tock" Rivulets of steaming hot water cascade down the sides of the bus. The wind begins to scream like a banshee.

"Tic, Tock!" The men on the bus begin to yell at the driver to turn around. The driver and guards ignore their pleas. Their heads face forward, not moving, like the dead.

"Tic, Tock!" The heat on their shackles begins to burn through the prisoners' skin. "We are almost there." The guard speaks in a monotone.

"Tic, Tock, Tic, Tock!" Stygian darkness falls. The road ahead begins to shift and crack. Sulfurous smoke rises to cover the bus. They begin to move faster and faster until the bus comes to a jarring halt, flinging the prisoners to the grime covered steel floor.

"Tic, Tock" Their final prison straight ahead, black like a thousand starless nights. The massive iron prison doors are flung wide; red-hot flames come searching from within, flickering, A man in a stark black cloak that hides his face walks from the black maw, pulls out his watch.

"TIC TOCK, TIC TOCK, TICK, TOCK! The flames are eager to serve him.

"Tic, Tock, Tic, Tock!" The prisoners walk down the bus stairs and stare with wild fear in their eyes.

"TIC TOCK, TIC, TOCK, TIC TOCK!" The man points forward and the flames hungrily find .their prey, shooting forward. They wrap around the figures like a lover's cape and drag them through the open darkness before them.

"TIC TOCK.....Tic Tock....tic tock....tic.............." The dark figure turns and follows the red flickering, dancing flames. As he enters the doors, he murmurs, "Welcome to Hell!" as the doors crash closed.

Author Biography

Louis Edwards

Louis Edwards has traveled around the world and lived in many countries. His experience and love for the Lord has helped him to minister to many people. Serving as a song leader, adult Sunday School teacher, and filling in as a minister brings him great joy.

He now lives in Eastern North Carolina, with his wife of 35 years, Roberta. He has two children and seven grandchildren.

Using the talent the Lord has given him, he has written many devotions that he uses on his blog and in church. His writing has helped and inspired many in their time of need. His greatest desire is to honor the Lord with his writing.

I can do all things through Christ which strengtheneth me. Phil. 4:13

July Writer's Challenge

The night is still young. Will it be a night of romance or a night of intrigue? Only your characters will know. Will you paint their paths, or will they lead you by the hand?

Haven

By Louis Edwards

Michael stood along the desolate highway staring at the ominous clouds overhead. Sharp penetrating tentacles of light streaked across the canvas of black, illuminating the hordes that loomed above the little town of Haven. He knew this mission would come at a cost. If he and his army failed, the town would lose all hope, and faith would be lost. He was thankful for his brothers in arms, Uriel and Kushiel. Like him, they were battle-hardened and ready to answer the call of their commander, Yahweh.

"My brothers," Michael looked at his two legionnaires. "Haven is under siege, and I think I may know who their leader is."

Kushiel spoke up. "Who?"

"The Prince of Persia."

Uriel and Kushiel drew their swords, raised them to the air and said in unison. "In the name of Yahweh, we will defeat him and his imps."

Michael raised his hand. "Put away your weapons; there'll be plenty of time for that later." He appreciated their zeal, but the battle would be fought on a different front this time. The enemy would be expecting them, and he didn't want another 28-day war like they had in Babylon.

He turned to Uriel and placed his hand on his shoulder. "Uriel, my brother, I need you to take a few of your host and go to the prayer warrior's house. Kushiel and I will create a diversion and draw the Prince of Persia and his minions away. Make sure you protect her at all cost. She must get through to the mayor."

Uriel drew his sword, slapped it across his chest and with a sharp snap he bowed his head. Michael returned the gesture and signaled for Kushiel to join him.

The two entered the town and stopped in front of the prayer warrior's house. The sentinels stationed around the house drew their swords.

Michael stood with his arms crossed. "Do you really think you can stop me?"

A gravelly voice broke through the chatter among the hoards guarding the house. "They may cower and run but I never will."

Michael grinned and looked at Kushiel. "I think we found him."

"Was there any doubt." Kushiel drew his sword and both of them turned their attention to the front door when the Prince of Persia materialized.

"So we meet again." A sinister grin crossed the Prince's face. "This time I have the upper hand. Look around you."

Michael looked around. He knew the enemy had a stronghold on Haven, but there was still hope as long as the prayer warrior didn't give up. "You'll never win this battle, and even if you do, Yahweh will have the final say."

The demon's eyes narrowed and his nostrils flared at the name of the one who made and controlled the universe. "We'll see about that."

The Prince yanked his sword from its sheath, sprang from the porch and aimed for Michael's neck. Michael ducked and signaled for Kushiel to follow him to lure the Prince and his minions away from the house.

The Prince barked, "After them, you imbeciles," and followed in pursuit.

Uriel watched from a distance, and when the enemy left the house, he and his host swooped in to take advantage of the moment. He instructed some of them to set up a perimeter while he and the others entered the building.

As they entered, Uriel caught a glimpse of movement from the corner of his eye and ducked in time to miss the blow of a sword. Before the demon could strike again, one of his team cut the vermin in half, sending him to the abyss. Chaos alerted the others in the house, causing a black mass of swirling demons to appear. While the two hosts battled, Uriel snuck into the kitchen where the Mayor and prayer warrior sat discussing the word of God.

Spotting his foe standing behind the mayor with his black talons wrapped over the man's shoulders, Uriel drew his sword. He knew his enemy wouldn't give up and the battle scars that marred his body told Uriel that this wasn't his first battle.

The beast drew his weapon and sliced through the air. "Do you think you're going to stop me?"

"I come in the name of Jehovah the mighty God of heaven and I will stop you." Uriel lunged toward the creature. Their swords clashed, and the sound of thunder filled the air. The beast unleashed a volley of blows that Uriel was able to ward off. With each pass, he could feel the heat from the searing sword.

Uriel could feel his strength increasing by the minute. He could tell by the mayor's expression his heart was getting softer, and the energy emanating from the prayer warrior filled the room. The blows from the demon grew weaker with each strike. Uriel scanned the beast's armor looking for a vulnerable spot.

###

Michael could feel the power and was thankful the Prince was so consumed with anger that he couldn't see his army slowly falling apart. Michael drew his sword. "You'll never win. You sealed your fate the day you decided to follow Lucifer."

The prince's scaly body grew darker and the scar that ran across his eye intensified as the demon glared at Michael. "I'll show you who's going to win." His voice filled the air like rolling thunder. Michael prepared himself for the evil that was about to be unleashed and instructed Kushiel to stand ready.

Uriel saw what he was looking for, a chink in his opponent's armor just under the fifth rib. He waited, and as the demon lunged forward, Uriel plunged his sword deep into the brute's chest. The adversary screamed and faded into a pile of black dust.

As the prince started to lunge, a brilliant light pierced the darkness overhead sending him and his host scattering like roaches. In one last cry, he said, "It's not over."

Michael and Kushiel joined Uriel, and the trio celebrated another victory over one more soul.

Author Biography

E. M. Satterley

The author -- that's me, above -- was born on Long Island, New York, which, by the way, happens to be the setting for my second historical novel, *Nowhere to Go.*

My wife, Cathy, and I are currently retired and living in North Carolina, close to the Atlantic coast.

We have three grown children and three grandchildren. How did I get into writing? Well, I've always been interested in writing and I've written a few things in the past, but now I have the opportunity and more time to share my talent with new friends and faithful readers.

Eddie Oops

By E. M. Satterley

Ah, 1960. Those were the days. Dad was assigned to Fort Devens, Massachusetts, as an ignition instructor, and the days for a twelve-year-old boy like me were carefree. Our family lived near a small New England town just a few miles from the Post in a newly painted barn-red house. It sat on a hill, and the dirt and stone driveway led to the double-car garage built underneath the house. My thirteen-year-old brother and I and a few neighbor boys spent our summer days hiding behind moss-covered boulders imagining we were cowboys or soldiers or just playing hide-and-seek. The farmer across the narrow country road did not seem to mind if we played in his pasture land. The only negative about playing there was that we had to look where we stepped. The cow pies were all around. Also, at the appropriate time of the year, we enjoyed running across the countryside finding wild blueberry bushes. We would always bring home enough of the blue ripened delicacies to add to our corn flakes for at least a couple of days.

One late, sunny afternoon, Dad called my brother Jim and me into the kitchen. I noticed right away that he was going to be telling the good news. On his garrison cap, he displayed a new set of captain's bars. They gleamed almost as bright as the smile on his face. "Eddie, Jimmy, I've got some good news." Mom was behind Jimmy holding our baby sister. "I've been promoted," he said proudly.

"Wow," Jimmy and I said together. I'm guessing that we weren't quite experienced enough to offer our congratulations, but we soon learned.

Mother stepped around and gave Dad a kiss on the cheek, "Congratulations, sweetheart."

"This means that there will be some changes around here," Dad continued.

I asked, "What do you mean, Dad?"

"First of all, I am raising your allowances."

I looked at Jimmy and we were both smiling. "Yep," Dad said, "now your allowance, Eddie, will be a dollar a week and Jimmy's will be a dollar and a quarter."

I felt a little slighted. I mean, Jimmy and I were only a year and a half apart, why did he get more money than me? When I looked at Jimmy's face again, he was sneering as though he was saying, *Ha ha, I'm getting more than you!* He was silent then but pushed it in my face later that day and for about a week afterward.

Curious, I asked, "What other changes?"

"You remember that little car that Mr. Hosington was selling? Well, I've decided to buy it."

The sports car was a classic British 1954 MG TF convertible. I remember Dad often retiring to the garage to work on his new toy. My dad was a perfectionist, and he wouldn't show the car off until it was in perfect condition. Near the end of the summer, Dad had the car almost completed. One last required item was a new glass taillight lens to replace the cracked one that came with the car. It was ordered over a month before from Lucas Electrical, an after-market electrical parts store. Dad was anxious to receive it not just so he could finish the project, but so he could then show it to his friends.

Then the day came when he received a call from the parts store in Ayer. "Your lens finally came in, Captain, will you be coming in today to pick it up?"

"What time do you close?"

"Three today, and we'll be open 'til six on Monday."

"I'll be right there, wait for me," Dad said with a look of urgency on his face. He didn't ask if anyone wanted to go with him, he just flew out of the house, into the family car, and then sped down the road out of sight.

An hour later, he pulled up the inclined driveway to the house. I happened to be at the window when he parked the car in the shade, tucked a small cardboard box under his arm, and opened the garage door to reveal the back of his pride and joy.

I ran down the inside stairs to meet him below. I found him rummaging through his toolbox looking for the perfect screwdriver.

"Hi, Dad! Did you get it?"

"Yeah, finally."

"Can I help?" I said.

Silence from Dad. I now surmise that he was thinking how to answer that question. *Really not much you can do, it's a one-man job. Besides, I wanted to finish...to put the last piece in place.*

As Dad unwrapped the lens from the box and packing paper, I also bent down to watch. "Here, hold this." Dad handed me the lens as he unscrewed the broken one from the light fixture and smoothed the rubber gasket with his fingers. Just as he motioned for the lens, it slipped from my hand and crashed to pieces on the cement floor. My heart pounded in my throat and my body flushed from head to toe. I was afraid to look Dad in the face.

"Oops," I said.

"Oops?" Dad repeated. I was expecting the worse. Yelling. Screaming. Maybe even a smack to the head. I was squeamishly avoiding his look and waiting for the eventual explosion.

But all he said was, "Oops?" I guess he counted to ten before he made any rash outburst choices. I was glad of that. In fact, even days later (and after he reordered the same part) it was not mentioned until he started calling me "Eddie Oops" on a regular basis. In fact, I was beginning to think that was my new name. Had I realized that for the next twenty years he would always refer to me as "Eddie Oops," I would have opted to stay upstairs when I saw him enter the garage on that fateful day.

Author Biography

Keenan Dupree

Keenan Dupree, known professionally as K. Dupree, is an author born in the Bronx, New York, in October of 1992. Soon after, his family moved to Prince George's County, Maryland, where he was raised. He currently lives with his mother and father, Sharon and Vincent Hayes, in Greenville, North Carolina. He began as a tyro writer in the third grade, where he received the initial push to write by his teacher, Mr. Victor Turner. Dupree enjoys reading, playing video games, watching movies, and writing. So far he's written one book—his first book—entitled *Boy from the Clouds*, and he looks forward to his many future published works.

Vim and Vigor

By Keenan Dupree

I'm comin', V. Just hold on, I'm comin', he thought to himself moving onto the highway.

It was dark and damp as he ran down the long, vacant stretch of road. The cold of the night air condensed his breath as he breathed vehemently to fuel his inhumanly strong body. Swiftly, his heart raced, but not just for him running the speed limit. He feared for his brother.

Is this the right way? he thought, checking his surroundings as he ran. *Did I take a wrong turn?*

Suddenly, he looked overhead as a bright flash caught his attention. It appeared as if a storm were brewing high in the dark clouds. He looked as lightning boomed and streaked across the black sky, and they were all flowing in the same direction—the direction he was running. Looking back down at the roadway as he reached the top of the cresting road, he saw the unnaturally bright lights of the city. He hurried his pace.

Once he reached the city, he could hear the wild crackle of electricity, and the boom of the thunder had grown much louder. From his location, he could see the lightning striking down into the city, disappearing behind the buildings. He winced through his goggles at the bright flashes.

"V, what are they doing to you?"

He continued on. Once in the heart of the city, looking up, he could see that the lightning was being drawn down by the antenna of the tallest building in the city. He looked back down at the front of the building and charged.

He ran straight through the glass door. He then took off for the stairs. The 100-floor building had a 1,482-stair climb but he could traverse them much faster than the elevator could lift him to the top, so he ran. He moved so swiftly that when he rounded the corners, he ran up onto the walls in a low arc. The booming and crackling grew louder as he neared the top. Then, suddenly, he began to hear screaming.

"VIM!" He cried as he hurried his already feverish pace.

He soon came to the door to the roof. It did not stand a chance.

He burst through, out onto the roof, and there on the roof, he saw his brother. He was locked in metal restraints to a metal chair attached to a lightning rod. He was being used as a generator. Usually, Vim could take and even withstand an influx of electricity, but because he was receiving so much at once, the process was killing him. Vigor spent no time thinking. He rushed over and grabbed Vim's restraints.

The massive electrical power surging in and through Vim's body and chair sent Vigor soaring. Straight back he flew, slamming into the second-to-last floor of the adjacent building. As he lay there on the floor, he opened his hands revealing a squeezed metal cuff and a large piece of the other cuff. Back on the roof, Vim had an arm free and was pulling desperately at the remaining cuff. As Vigor came to, shuddering from the residual effects of the electrocution, he was greeted most unwelcomely.

"I hate drones."

They were small, shiny, dark, metallic, flying spheres, about the size of a volleyball.

"Ow!"

And they shot lasers. Vigor dove out of the way then rolled onto his feet. The drones were coming at Vigor from the other building, through the window he had just crashed through. He ran at them and leaped. Stepping on each of them lightly and briefly, he hopped, skipped, and jumped his way back over to the roof of the other building. But just before he could stick the landing, all of the drones turned and fired on him.

Vigor went flying forward, landing on his face. Then, swiftly, as he stood to his feet, he plunged his hands into the roof and pulled up a chunk of the roof itself. He then turned and hurled it at the nearest drone. It crashed into the drone hard, putting a large scrape on the side of its armor plating and knocking it for a loop. It spun around violently and crashed into another, blowing up both in the process. Suddenly, another drone swooped in for him, rapidly firing blast after blast. He jumped at it and snatched it out of the air, crushed it in his hands, and hurled it at another.

Just then, hearing him yell out once more, Vigor turned and ran for his brother. As Vigor swiftly approached, Vim noticed his brother running toward him. In between jolts from the lightning rod, Vim managed to focus his mind and his energy. He then stretched out his hand and blasted the remaining drones with a bolt of lightning that forked out to hit each one of them. Vigor reached Vim and grabbed the remaining restraint. He roared as the massive electrical energy surged through his body, fighting to free his brother from the torment of the machine. The metal began to yield under his great strength. Then, it finally gave. He snatched the leg restraints off like they were paper, seized Vim, and hoisted him out of the chair. Almost immediately, the machine that was seconds ago so lively, was now inactive and silent. Vigor dropped to his knees with Vim over his shoulder, then set Vim down in front of him. He was breathing heavily. He was propping himself up with one hand on the ground while the other stayed hooked around Vigor's shoulders. Vigor himself had an arm around Vim's ribs holding him up, with the other hand on his chest giving support.

"Vig... Vig...," said Vim between breaths.

"Don't talk. Get your wind back first," said Vigor.

Vim breathed. He was exhausted. Vigor, kneeling there with him, rubbed his back in an attempt to soothe him and ease him through the initial recovery period. After a time, Vim's breathing slowed. He lifted his hand up off the ground and patted Vigor twice on the shoulder briefly.

"Thank you, Vig... Thank you...."

"I've got your back, little brother."

Vim's hand went back to the ground, heavy. He continued to breathe deep.

"Just rest. We'll get whoever did this when you can stand. And this time...we'll stand together."

Author Biography

Sherri Hollister

Sherri Lupton Hollister is the recent chairperson for the Pamlico Writer's Group. She loves everything about writing from the first glimmer of an idea to the final product. Reading, reviewing, discussing and learning about other writers and their process has helped develop her own writing. Sherri writes romantic suspense set in a small Southern town. She lives with her own romantic hero, her husband of more than 25 years. Together they raised six sons and will soon welcome their eighteenth grandchild. Sherri hopes to publish the first book in her series, *Chrome Pink,* this spring.

August Writer's Challenge

For a brief moment, you catch a glimpse of someone in the shadows. Who is he? What does he want? He disappears only to reappear when you least expect him to.

Nightmare

By Sherri Hollister

The echo of footsteps on the sidewalk made it feel as if I were inside a brass bell. The sound surrounded me but I could see no one for the fog. I could barely see my hand in front of my face. It was late, near midnight, and I'd thought the streets were empty until I heard the footsteps. I sped up. Whoever was behind me increased his speed as well. My heart pounded in my chest. My mouth was dry. Should I call out? Perhaps, like me, someone is going home late and is frightened by the fog. No sound would emerge from my constricted throat. The night was deprived of sound; only the heaviness of my breathing and the reverberation of footsteps behind me disturbed the silence. I ducked my head and hurried up the street.

The night was alive with smoke and shadows, swirling around me, like a gray cloak. Was it protecting me, or making it easier for my stalker to prey? I did not dare veer from my usual path for fear I could not remember my way without light or landmark. I slowed my pace as the night became darker. The silence descended, oppressive and suffocating. My thoughts whirled with demons, devils, and assorted evil folk both real and lore.

I shuddered as shapes materialized out of the fog. A man in a hat with a big cigar gained substance, flesh made from smoke. But like smoke, he vanished as my feet stalled. Was he real or a mirage? Perhaps just a shade. Surely no man made of bone could have vanished so swiftly?

The scent of his tobacco lingered in the night air. A memory stirred within my fevered brain. Who smoked such sweet cigars? Do I dare call his name? For if it is he, that one from my thoughts, it must be a ghost. I dared not ask for fear it was the truth. The shadow that hunted me this night was the one whom I'd just left, dead in his room.

Author Biography

Gloria Loftin

I have been writing since I was five years old. That is my first love. I am also a voracious reader. I live in Grimesland, NC. We moved here in 2005 from Northern Virginia. I missed out on college when I was younger. My parents had four children to support. My parents could not afford to send me to college at that time.

I had my chance when I asked my mom and dad if they would pay for me to go to college at the age of 6, and they said yes. I missed out when I was younger, but I believe that I appreciated it more at that age. Now I just love to learn, something I did not care for as a teenager.

I am unpublished but hope to remedy that soon. I have found a wonderful group of people who support and encourage every chance they get.

Thank you for the time to get to know me a little better.

September Writer's Challenge

Are they looking for you? You really didn't mean it to happen that way. Maybe, this is your first job and you were hoping for that big break. Everyone looks suspicious.

A Second Chance

By Gloria Loftin

His friends made fun of him—a police captain working at the mall. He had a family to feed and many relatives as well. When they laughed at him, he just stood up tall and proud and ignored their taunts.

It had been a long day at the Valley Mall. It was Christmastime, and children were running around, some getting lost or jumping in the fountains, or screaming at the top of their lungs to see Santa.

The parents scowled at him as if it was his fault for their precious offsprings' behavior.

Almost quitting time, he thought. *Time to head back to the Mall office to clock out. Tomorrow is Christmas Eve.* And he wanted to spend every minute that he could with his family.

"Jim, can I see you a moment?" his boss asked. Jim walked over to him. "Can you work the graveyard shift? Bob called in sick."

Jim sighed deeply but said okay. He knew that Bob's wife was having a bad pregnancy, and he was worried sick that something would happen to her. She was due any day.

As the Mall emptied and the lights went out, Jim left the office for his hourly round of store watching. He passed many fine stores that he wished he could shop at, for his wife and family.

This was going to be a lean Christmas because the doctor's bills for his youngest were reaching $200,000 and the insurance would not pay the whole amount for the surgery that his son needed to stay alive. Jim didn't care if he had to work three or four jobs; he was going to make sure that his family was intact and healthy.

His son, Danny, had been born with a weak heart and they were still waiting for a donor. Jim prayed every night to be strong for his family, but he cried sometimes when he was alone, like now. He hated that another child had to die for his son to live.

As he started on his second circuit of the Mall, he saw a white light and then heard a voice coming from Santa's Village. He walked over and saw a young boy with the brightest eyes he had ever seen, almost inhuman, sitting in Santa's chair.

"Son, what are you doing here, and where are your parents?"

"I don't know," he said. "I was in the car with my parents and we were singing Christmas carols and now I am here."

"What is your name?"

"Aiden," the boy replied.

Jim's phone began to ring. "Hello," he said. His wife was shouting for him to come to the hospital right now. They had found a donor for their son. Jim's heart began to race as he ran for the Mall office. Just then he remembered the boy in Santa's Village, but when he went back he was gone. Jim searched for him, but could not find him anywhere. He was beginning to wonder if the boy was real or if he just imagined him.

When he got to the hospital, there was a family in the waiting room crying. The mother was holding a picture of her son. Jim glanced over and was shocked to see that it was the boy, Aiden, from the Mall.

He and his wife went in to see Danny before the surgery. He looked pale, but always with a sweet smile on his face and the deepest brown eyes in the universe, at least that is what Jim thought.

"Did Aiden find you?" Danny asked.

Before Jim could ask Danny what he meant, the doctor said, "It's time, sport, time to get you a new racing engine." They kissed and hugged Danny, and off he went.

Jim and his wife went back to the waiting room, and Aiden's family was still there. They had been told that their son's heart was going to a very sick little boy. Aiden's mother looked at Jim and his wife. With tears in her eyes, she walked over to them and asked if she could speak to them. Of course, they said yes.

Jim asked, "Is that a picture of your son, Aiden?

The woman looked at him in shock. "How did you know?"

"I'm a police captain and a security guard at the Valley Mall. Aiden was sitting on a chair in Santa's Village. I asked him what he was doing there and he told me a fantastic story."

Aiden's mother told Jim and his wife that Aiden had always been a special little boy, wise beyond his years. They had adopted him as a baby and from the first, he seemed to know things. He said that he would have a brother, but we were not able to have children and were getting too old to adopt. "He is, was, our only child."

Jim told them about Danny asking if he had talked to Aiden.

"He had a secret friend named Danny, but we thought that was just his imagination," Aiden's mom said. They sat there and talked about both of their exceptional sons for hours.

The doctor came into the waiting room and told him that Danny was looking fine and they could see him in a couple of hours.

Jim asked Aiden's parents to stay with them. They agreed. When Danny was able to see his parents, Jim asked if they would like to see him also.

They walked into Danny's room. Both parents stood on each side of Danny's bed. He opened his eyes and smiled with a look beyond his years. He had one deep brown eye and one bright blue one.

Miracles do happen at Christmas!

The Anthology Team

The anthology composition team includes Pamlico Writers' Group member editors Doris Schneider and Jeanne Julian, formatting by James Keen, cover design by Louis Edwards, and oversight by Sherri Hollister.

Numerous hours were required for compiling the book. As part payment for those hours, the following entries by the team are included.

Author Biography

Doris Schneider

Doris was born in Texas and lived all over the U.S. and Canada. After 33 years of teaching theatre at William Carey University in Hattiesburg, Mississippi and North Carolina Central University in Durham, Doris retired to little Washington where she paints, designs jewelry, plays the violin and writes.

Doris has published two novels, *Borrowed Things* and *By Way of Water,* and has short stories in the anthology, *A Carolina Christmas.* She is currently seeking publication for her novella, *Drummer Girl.*

Her time is divided between the North Carolina coast and the mountains, where her husband Jim Coke raises wildflowers.

Scary Story

By Doris Schneider

My journaling teacher asked us to write a scary story. I had trouble thinking of a story or event that really scared me. I'm sure frightening things happened; I just couldn't remember them. My daughter and granddaughters visited over the weekend. So, I asked them.

The six-year-old said, "I got nothing, Nana."

The nine-year-old told me stories she heard in camp about dolls coming to life and killing whole families. That rang a bell. It reminded me that, as a child, I'd had a recurring dream of my dolls coming to life and terrifying me. But that's it—end of story. However, I think the scariest thing about dolls coming to life is that the current robotic technology mixed with cloning might actually make it happen.

So, looking at my beautiful granddaughters, I thought in a different direction. There is a fear I have had, even when I was very young. It is the fear of a child being kidnapped. I have always felt that is perhaps the most terrifying thing a parent could endure. I knew that I did not want to become rich because excessive money might make my children a more likely target for ransom.

Happily, I've never been rich or worried about a missing child. But those thoughts reminded me of a truly scary story.

When I was in the fourth grade and my brother was in the fifth, we lived in LaPorte, Texas. Our parents wanted to go out one evening, so they dropped us off at the movie theatre, an inexpensive babysitter. I don't remember the movie, but I'm sure we watched it at least twice, each of us eventually sliding down in our chair, fast asleep, where we remained until the wee hours of the morning.

In the earlier evening, Mama and Daddy had returned from their honkytonking date to find the theatre dark and locked. There had been a mixup about the movie schedule, and they arrived an hour after the theatre closed. They drove all around the area, looking for us before contacting the police. They even stopped other cars to ask if they had seen us. This was long before AMBER Alerts and immediate action to search for missing children. The police were called.

Finally, our parents found someone driving by who said they had seen two kids walking up by the San Jacinto Monument—miles away. They drove there—no luck.

In the meantime, Tommy woke up first and then shook me awake. It was creepy, looking around us and seeing only empty seats and very dim light. Tommy took my hand, and we walked into the concession area, also empty and dim. He was probably plotting our escape from the locked theatre, while I was contemplating popcorn for breakfast with serious enthusiasm. So, I was disappointed when I saw him open the main door which was locked from the outside but not from the inside.

Again, he grabbed my hand, pulled me away from the popcorn, and we walked out onto the sidewalk and empty street, still half asleep, unsure of what to do next. Then we saw headlights rounding the corner. A car pulled up. The passenger door opened, and Mama ran to us, crying and hugging, and crying and hugging, and crying. Daddy was slumped over the steering wheel, probably whispering one of his rare but sincere prayers.

I have a vague recollection of a police car pulling up, and upon seeing us, pulling away again—kids found, case closed. I remember thinking the whole thing was funny. But there was no laughter in our parents, and they never let a movie babysit us again.

Mama and Daddy had experienced hours of what I have since feared—the mind-wrenching horror of someone taking your child. So, this was not my scary story. It was theirs.

Author Biography

James Keen

A Pamlico Writers' Group member since 2008, I have served as Chairman.

I have written two newspaper columns chronicling my sailing adventures: *Nautical Musings*, a weekly column about family adventures on the coast; and *In the Loop,* a bi-weekly column featuring adventures while crossing the Atlantic.

My book *Trinidad Express* is a detailed chronicle of the 5,300 mile doublehanded South Africa to Trinidad Atlantic crossing. My ebook, *Log of S/V Irish Mist* chronicles my singlehanded 13-month, 6,000-mile circumnavigation of the eastern United States, an adventure named "America's Great Loop." *Nautical Musings I and II* are ebook anthologies of my newspaper articles.

Newspaper Route Driving Lessons

By James Keen

My passion for genealogy research often triggers pleasant memories of family times. I'm reminded of how grateful I am to be a part of a loving and honorable past. Recently, a memory of the family newspaper route where I learned to drive came to mind.

It was not unusual in the 1950s for a man to have a second job to supplement the family income. My maternal grandparents were farmers with a longtime second job as rural newspaper carriers for the Raleigh *News and Observer*. They helped Dad secure a similar route to add to income from his farm machinery sales business. The new route was in an adjoining county, just a short drive south of our home.

The U.S. Postal Service provided weekday rural newspaper delivery on Dad's route. Bundles of papers fresh off the late evening printing press were delivered to the Raleigh post office where efficient postal service trucks scattered them to far-flung areas. Rural mail carriers included the newspaper among their normal delivery that same day.

However, the bulging Sunday newspaper had eight to ten sections and was overstuffed with colorful commercial inserts until it often reached a four-inch thickness. It was too large for postal service delivery and required Dad to deliver that monster along his route.

Dad's routine included a monthly all-day collection and sales trek where he combined collecting for newspapers from customers and farm machinery selling to prospective clients. Each Sunday, he delivered newspapers to customer's driveways and mailboxes.

Dad started his nighttime route about two a.m. on Sunday morning by meeting a large delivery truck at a local service station. He would fold down the back seat of the family V-8 powered, 1955 Plymouth Suburban station wagon, and load large bundles of papers. After driving into the adjoining county, he tossed papers onto customer driveways or stuffed them into mailboxes. Near the southernmost point of the route, he arrived at another newspaper carrier's house where half of the remaining paper bundles were offloaded into the carrier's car for delivery. Along dad's return route, he delivered a stack of newspapers to an all-night diner where he would visit with patrons while having a cup of coffee and a snack. If the weather cooperated, dad would finish the route about seven a.m.

Washing road grime and smashed bugs from the station wagon was an early morning chore that Dad insisted on doing before joining mom and family for breakfast. We'd dress in Sunday clothes and ride in a clean car to Sunday school and church. In the afternoon, the family rode in that trusty shiny station wagon for a big Sunday lunch at one of our nearby grandparent's homes. It was a long day for dad who often had a recliner nap after a hearty meal.

Early in the paper route experience, Dad decided that he needed help and recruited my brother and me. Our job was to wrap newspapers, usually just one thick fold, and secure it with one or more stout rubber bands. In rainy weather, we would insert the paper into a plastic wrapper.

My brother or I would sit in the front passenger seat to toss papers into driveways or stuff them into mailboxes. The other helper wrapped papers while sitting in the back seat surrounded by hefty paper bundles. We became accomplished in our tasks and alternated chores. After completing the long route, we usually got to sleep a bit on the drive home. However, we were expected to participate in the car washing ritual.

The next challenge on the newspaper route came when I was old enough to get a driver's learner permit. I had driven a tractor around dad's farm machinery business from a very young age as a fun and expected skill while helping around the business. The nighttime paper route offered almost deserted roads to upgrade my driving skills from tractors to cars. However, dodging frequent road-crossing deer and opossum was a challenge. I never hit a deer, but I did squash a few opossums in their amble across the road.

School driver training sessions helped me learn facts necessary to pass the license test. It also forced me to learn skills necessary to interact with girls trapped with me within the school training car. I learned to safely drive in the heavier traffic around our small town.

Returning to my memory, the Plymouth station wagon had a manual gear shift that caused a bit of a problem. However, after stopping and starting at mailboxes countless times, shifting gears became routine.

Dodging mailboxes was more of a problem. The driver would bounce through roadside mud puddles to maneuver the front car fender under the mailbox and position the opening just inches from the passenger window. If the driver stopped the car too far from the mailbox, the helper had to open the car door to reach the mailbox. Stopping too close resulted in a dinged window post. I admit that I misjudged the distance a few times with resulting scratches.

The route was monotonous as we mastered the rhythm of throwing papers or placing them into the boxes. We always got relief and a treat at the all-night diner before the long drive home when dad had time to sleep while I drove.

I fell asleep once and allowed the car to wander across the center line. Inexperience caused me to oversteer in correction and skid sideways along the road. Dad had some rare sharp words to say that night. His message was so strong that today, after nearly sixty years of driving, I can say I have not again fallen asleep behind the steering wheel.

It is a pleasure to remember how Dad used his newspaper route to teach his sons valuable lessons of hard work in early morning hours. The driving lessons were a bonus.

Thank you, Dad!

Author Biography

Louis Edwards

Louis Edwards has traveled around the world and lived in many countries. His experience and love for the Lord has helped him to minister to many people. Serving as a song leader, adult Sunday School teacher, and filling in as a minister brings him great joy.

He now lives in Eastern North Carolina, with his wife of 35 years, Roberta. He has two children and seven grandchildren.

Using the talent the Lord has given him, he has written many devotions that he uses on his blog and in church. His writing has helped and inspired many in their time of need. His greatest desire is to honor the Lord with his writing.

I can do all things through Christ which strengtheneth me. Phil. 4:13

Full Circle

By Louis Edwards

Jake eased down on the gas pedal of his '57 Chevy and wrung the steering wheel with his hands. The crisp autumn air and scenic route of the Blue Ridge Parkway did little to ease the pain that ripped through his heart. Searing images and painful words of Johnny's tragic death five years ago ate at him like a cancer. It wasn't that he didn't want his son to get married; he just wanted him to finish school. His wife Mary Lou tried to convince him it wasn't his fault, but how could he persuade himself?

He eased his car off the road onto a little turnout overlooking the parkway. It was empty, which was unusual for this time of year. Maybe the time alone would help him sort things out. He exited the car, walked to the metal barrier separating beauty from danger, and propped his forearms against the top rail. Admiring the scenery, he sighed, "Mary Lou, I wish you were here. You were always the one with the level head." He swallowed hard and the canvas of colors in the valley started running together.

It seemed like just yesterday he and Johnny were up here laughing and kidding with one another. They had just finished restoring the '57 Chevy, and Johnny kept pestering him about driving the car. Jake dangled the keys in front of him, and they wrestled for a while until wisdom gave in to youth. Jake tried pushing the memory from his mind and lifted his glasses to wipe the pain from his eyes. If only it were that easy.

Out of the corner of his eye, he noticed a young man approaching the turnout. The intruder couldn't have been more than 23. His shoulder length brown hair, tattered jeans, denim jacket, and backpack reminded Jake of a freeloader trekking across the country. Jake wasn't in the mood for company, especially a bum.

The young man approached the barrier and lowered his pack to the ground. Jake refused to make eye contact, hoping the invader would leave and let him wallow in his self-pity. It wasn't long before the young man encroached on Jake's space by trying to start a conversation.

"It's beautiful up here."

Jake refused to answer, hoping the kid would get the hint.

The stranger continued, "Do you come up here often?"

Jake stood straight and grabbed the railing. "I used to come up here with my wife and son."

The young man settled against the railing. Jake turned his attention back to the swaying trees below and hoped this would end the inquisition. The searing words he spoke before his son's accident continued to haunt him. *If you leave, don't you ever come back.* He regretted the venom that spewed from his mouth that night. If he could only take them back, his son would be here today.

The stranger looked at Jake and smiled. "You know, only God could make something like this so beautiful."

Jake tried to ignore the kid, but the young man's carefree spirit made it difficult. It was something he missed about his son. "Yeah, Johnny used to say the same thing when we came up here." His voice trailed off and he swallowed hard.

"I'm sorry, I didn't mean to pry."

"It's okay." He chided himself for being so cold; the problem wasn't with the young man, but with the guilt that strangled his heart. Maybe Mary Lou was right, he should get on with his life and quit blaming himself and staying mad at the world.

The young man picked up his pack and slung it over his shoulder. "Well, sir. It's been good, and I hope you have a nice day."

"You too."

Jake turned and watched the young man disappear around the bend. He couldn't escape the nagging idea that he should help the kid. Why should he? The boy probably wanted to be alone. Who knows, maybe he's running from something or someone. In the back of his mind, he could hear his wife prodding. *Jake, why don't you help the boy? He could use the company and so could you?* He heaved a deep breath and looked at the sky. "What are you trying to do to me?"

Jake climbed into the car, cranked it, and turned on the eight-track player with *John Denver's Greatest Hits.* He put the car in gear and started up the winding parkway. If everything went right, the kid would accept the ride, keep his mouth shut, and he'd drop him off when he reached the cabin. As he rounded the curve, he spotted the young man and slowed the car to his pace.

"Hey, do you want a lift?" Jake hoped the kid would refuse.

"No, I'm okay. I've only got a few miles to go."

"Suit yourself." Jake started back up the parkway and stopped a few hundred feet down the road. He slammed his hand against the steering wheel, pulled off the road, and waited for the kid. He must be losing his mind. The kid didn't want a ride so why was he stopping? It couldn't be because he wanted company. He looked at the picture of his wife clipped to the sun visor. "Why are you making me do this?"

The young man approached the car and stuck his head in the window. "Is everything okay, mister?"

"Get in the car and throw your stuff in the back." Jake pointed to the back seat with his thumb.

"I'm okay, mister."

"Come on, you look like you could use a lift." He couldn't believe he was saying that.

"Thanks, I don't want to put you out."

"Yeah, well don't worry about it." If he had his way he never would have picked him up in the first place.

The young man opened the door, threw his pack in the back and climbed into the car. They eased back onto the parkway and the bumps in the road kept perfect time with the music. Jake noticed the young man tapping his foot and slapping the side of his leg, keeping tempo with the song *Country Roads*. He remembered how much his son loved that song. As the song ended and switched to another track, Jake decided to introduce himself.

"My name's Jake." He extended his hand to the young man.

The kid reached over and shook Jake's hand. "My friends call me Mac."

"Where you headed?" It was really none of Jake's business, but if he was going to make the best of this trip, there was no reason to act so cold toward the kid. It wasn't his fault.

"Home."

Jake felt a little uneasy asking when he saw the kid turn toward the window and wipe his face with the back of his hand. He decided it would be better not to prod unless the kid wanted to talk. Even then, Jake didn't want to open himself up to any scrutiny.

"You know," the young man kept looking out the side window, "I was nineteen when I left home and haven't been back since. I just hope that when I get there my dad will be glad to see me."

Jake would give anything to see his son again and feel his embrace. Why had he pushed him away? How could he ever forgive himself? His mind drifted for a moment. *Mary Lou, if I could only tell him I love him.*

They rounded the next curve and Jake spotted the mountain home he and his wife had shared. He stopped the car and looked at his passenger. "Well, this is as far as I go."

The rider shook Jake's hand, gathered his things, and got out of the car. "Thank you for the ride mister."

As the young man started to leave, Jake called out, "Hey kid."

The man returned to the car and leaned into the window. "Yeah?"

"Look, I know you don't know me, but when you do see your dad, make sure you tell him you love him and give him a hug. It'll mean more to him than you know."

"Thanks, I'll do that."

Jake watched the kid until he faded over the next hill. Even though they hadn't talked much, he felt the young man was on a similar journey, a path that would bring healing, hope, and reunion. In his own way, he knew today would begin a new chapter in his own life. He had to put it all behind him and start living.

Jake started down the gravel drive leading to the cabin. He was tired and wanted to be alone. Tonight he would do what his wife had suggested. He would write a letter to his son, tell him how he felt, and bury it in the backyard. With any luck, that would bring closure and ease the pain.

He parked in front of the cabin and sat there for a moment. The empty building called like sirens beckoning a wounded soul, one that longed to be filled with life, happiness, and peace. He got out of the car and opened the door to the vacant dwelling. The stale air was a stark reminder of the years he'd tried to put behind him.

After opening a few windows to revive the building, he removed the sheets from the furniture and piled them in a corner. He made his way to the kitchen and put on a pot of coffee before gathering a pen and legal pad. After pouring himself a cup, he settled in a chair at the end of the kitchen table.

Where would he start? What would he say? The last words he'd said were so final; a death sentence that couldn't be taken back. He rested his head in his hands. The emotions that had been bottled up for so long erupted into a torrent of tears that streamed down his face and onto the paper below. After he regained some composure, he started writing a letter that he hoped would ease the pain that tore him apart.

Dear Son,

The day you were born was the proudest day of my life. I knew you were someone special from the moment I held you in my arms. The times we had together brought great joy to my soul. I knew that one day you would want to spread your wings and fly. I just wasn't ready for it to be so soon.

Son, I'm so sorry for the things I said that night and wish there was some way I could take it all back. I want you to know that I never meant what I said. I would give anything to see you and hold you in my arms once again. I know you can't see what I'm writing, but I hope you are looking down from heaven and know that I love and miss you. If you can find it in your heart, will you please forgive me for what I have done? If you can't, I understand.

Love,

Dad

Somehow the words weren't enough to describe how he really felt, but it was the best he could do. His wife was right, putting it on paper helped to some degree, but it didn't completely ease the pain. Only time could mend a broken heart. His wife once told him, "Jake, hold onto the good times and let the bad fade away." He needed that now more than ever.

He rummaged through the cabinet, found a small cookie tin, and placed the letter in it. After retrieving a shovel from the utility building, he went to an old oak tree in the backyard with a rope swing hanging from it and buried the box. Exhausted from the emotional pain and years of regret, Jake decided to call it a night. Tomorrow would be a new day and he would try and get on with his life.

Jake woke up just as the sun poked its lazy head over the horizon. He pulled back the curtains and admired the view. It reminded him of a new start. The pain was still there, but he would learn to overcome it. He got dressed, went to the kitchen and started another pot of java before unloading the car.

As he removed his things from the back seat, he spotted an envelope on the floor. He picked it up and noticed there was no forwarding or return address. The kid must have lost it when he tossed his backpack in the car. He gathered his things along with the piece of mail he found and went into the house. After placing his belongings on the couch, he went to the kitchen and poured himself a cup of coffee.

Grabbing the letter, he went to the back patio and sat in a deck chair. He didn't cherish the idea of reading someone else's mail, but maybe it would give him an idea of where he could send it. He carefully opened it, removed a single page, and the first words he noticed were, "Dear Dad." They pierced his heart like an arrow striking a bullseye. He followed the handwritten script looking for clues but was stunned by its content.

Dear Dad,

It's been a long time since we talked, and I'm sorry for the way I left home. I hope you can forgive me for the pain I've caused you. Although I was only allowed to be with you a short time on the road, I can't wait until me, you, and mom can be together. I want you to know, I've always loved you and always will. You are the best dad I could ever ask for.

Your Son,

Johnny McDowell

The words ran together like ripples in a reflecting pool. Jake looked toward the last place he saw Johnny vanish over the horizon. Silhouetted against the sky was a small cloud shaped like praying hands, a gentle reminder sent from heaven of an answered prayer.

A healing balm had been applied to Jake's broken heart; even though the scars would remain, the pain would soon be a distant memory. For the first time, Jake felt his son's presence, a closeness he had longed for since Johnny's death. Now Jake's life had meaning, and one day he'd be reunited with his son.

"Producing stories and poems may not be a good way to make a living, but it's a wonderful way to make a life."

—Doris Betts, UNC-Chapel Hill

Made in the USA
Columbia, SC
19 November 2017